forwardpress

Forward Press Poets 2009

Eastern England

Edited by Forward Press Editors

First published in Great Britain in 2009 by:
Forward Press
Remus House
Coltsfoot Drive
Peterborough
PE2 9JX
Telephone: 01733 890099
Website: www.forwardpress.co.uk

SB ISBN 978-1-84418-510-8

Foreword

Here at Forward Press our aim has always been to provide a bridge to publication for as many undiscovered poets as possible. We firmly believe that poetry should be accessible to all and most importantly should connect with the reader. Over the past 21 years we have published a hugely diverse range of poems from writers young and old, creating anthologies that celebrate the wealth of writing talent on offer. With the inclusion of both traditional rhymes and more modern verse, there is always something to suit everyone's tastes.

This latest collection of poems written with creative flair and a passion for the local area is sure to engage and entertain. We hope you agree that Forward Press Poets 2009 - Eastern England is one to treasure and return to time and again.

Contents

The Poems

It Touched My Heart

I have travelled to many countries
Witnessed some wondrous sights
Met delightful people
Been in awe of the sun at midnight

I have walked up majestic mountains
Paddled in ice-melt streams
Ate delicious wild mountain strawberries
Topped with exotic ice creams

But there's a place which touched my heart
So deeply it feels part of me
It's the wilderness of Alaska
Where the land is pristine and free

The beauty is just pure magic
The glaciers give you a thrill
I long to recapture this spectacle
In my heart, I know that I will

The land belongs to the wildlife
The snow is untouched, so white
The air - so pure you can sense it
Blue crystals glint in the light

While watching the glaciers calving
Breathing in the cool crisp air
Glimpse seals floating by on icebergs
I felt privileged just to be there

My eyes fill with tears of emotion
Feeling blessed to have witnessed this sight
Never wanting the moment to finish
Just to stay until day turns to night.

Mary Webber

The Lark Ascending

The lark was singing way up high
Under a grey and sombre sky,
The rain had no way dampened his spirit
From Heaven this bird found his lyric.
Sweet pure notes make joyous the day
This bird's in no hurry to fly away.
The lark ascending, pure of note
Trilling from that tiny throat,
Soaring high above the wheat
Seems to me he's there to greet
Folk like us just passing by
From his viewpoint up on high.
To hear him is a joy to me
The lark ascending, glory be.

Lillian New

My Prayer

Let the deaf hear the music of kindness
Let the blind see the true Christian's light
Let the dumb speak of caring and sharing
To those in despair bring delight
To the poor a hope of the future
And courage for those who are ill
May frightened folk feel more secure
And acknowledge thy 'Peace be still'
Perhaps there is something that I can do
With this small humble being of mine
To dispel all the gloom and make the clouds go
Rainbow promises soon then will shine
Take me and show me and use me
Give me the right words to say
May I be their inspiration
This is my prayer Lord today.

Daphne M Brady

Always Press Forward

They have spread the word for twenty-one years,
Relaying those poetic joys and tears
Of writers who like to record their times,
With deep, sincere thoughts which blossom in rhymes

Without those steadfast encouraging souls
The words would be destined for coal-black holes,
Where the light of progress is rarely seen
But support and help can brighten the scene

We are not Shakespeare or even John Donne,
But having finished what we had begun
Brings an inner warmth to a lonely heart,
The words describe our life, or just a part

Yet knowing that we may appear in print
Brings to some aging eyes a useful glint,
So we press forward with our growing themes
Hoping that these words will enhance our dreams

And so that light is there for all to see
Knowing our work is viewed professionally,
While the verse is given the final test
We hope that ours may be one of those blessed

But whether we triumph or sadly lose
Our instincts are with those judges who choose
The descriptive words from an eager mind,
Which with an effort gradually unwind

And so we offer our comments to you
To decide who appears in your review,
For through the dark there is always a light
And a few chosen words could make it bright.

Doug Thomas

Ode To A Toad

Have you ever thought what it's like
Being a common or garden toad?
Who quakes at the sound of a Flymo,
Never mind trying to cross the road.
They call me bufo, bufo,
A harmless amphibian that's me,
So why do folks scream when I wander,
Do I look like a bad-tempered bee?
I live in a very big compost heap,
A rather smelly but attractive abode,
Which I share with a number of beetles
And a smaller less friendly toad.
I'm not very partial to vegetables
Or pieces of mouldy pie,
But they do attract my supper,
A most delicious, full-bodied fly.
They say I'm squat and dumpy,
That's really pretty unkind,
When I look at myself in the water
I'm delighted at what I find.
A bit on the plump side, I grant you
And I do have a wart or two,
But Mrs Toad says, I'm easily fancied
When I put myself on view.
So take care when you prod the woodpile
With that vicious old garden fork,
I'm not a fast runner, you know
At times I can hardly walk.
I do like a little siesta
If the sun is overly bright,
But I'm all about when the stars come out
And I dine rather well at night.
So when slugs drill holes in your hostas
And snails use your swede for a road,
Remember how useful I am to you,
Your friend, the humble toad.

Margaret Callow

No Light

Very slowly, she opens her eyes.
A teardrop gently falls on her cheek
She feels tired, helpless,
So deathly weak.

An empty silence fills the room
A cloud of darkness overshadows her mind
Her heart is thumping, pulsating her chest,
Lying quietly, glad of the rest.

Blood rushing through her ears
Trembling and nauseous and now rhythmic tears
Bright colours on her torso,
Shades of blue turning green.

The marks premeditated so as not to be seen
The pain she wears on her face
But too clever for that
No scars, not a visible trace.

The candle flickers on the floor
Drawn to the flame like a moth
But always one eye on the door.

Now delirious and ravenous
Going back to the past
A match made in Heaven
Surely to last.

Now back to reality
Afraid for her life
She'd always been a good loving wife.

Afraid to go, afraid to stay
Life was waiting,
Must find a way.

Get away from this inhuman callous being
The one she'd once loved
But would now be fleeing.

A prisoner of abuse
It rips you apart
Until there is only an empty heart.

Cheryl Field

Old Age And Memories

Where have all the years gone?
I've watched them fade away
Once I had so much time
There's little left today.
But I've many memories
Now that I'm getting old
The winter mornings bright and cold
Harvest fields of burnished gold.
That brilliant sun of summer dawn
The fretful wail of my first born
Muddy footprints down the hall
Cries of joy as bat hit ball.
Picnics outside in the sun
All those things we did for fun.
Winter evenings making toast
Birthday cards in the post.
Summer train rides to the coast
Spades and buckets in their hands.
To build castles on the sand
Collecting seashells to take back home
Tangled hair smoothed with a comb.
Christmas stockings - little treasures
Gave the children so much pleasure.
All the parties and the fun
With my daughters and my son.
It's so nice now to sit and dream
Of all the places that we've been.
I know, could I have my life again
That I would choose to do the same.

Peggy Montgomery

The Star

One night, as I was looking at the star-covered sky, admiring their splendour,
One star began to move away from the others and slowly, slowly moved closer to
the Earth.
The nearer it grew, the bigger it became.
It seemed as though the star was heading towards me.
Finally, the star landed near my feet with the lightness of a feather.
To my great surprise, the beautiful star began to speak,
'I came to you because I wish you to
Take a message of peace and love to the rest of the world.
I am the same star that many years ago
On Christmas night led the Three Kings to baby Jesus.
Jesus preached peace and faith to all the world
And I would like His word to be spoken
In all languages and to reach all humanity.
Tell everyone that the peace and the love have been
And will always be stronger than the hatred and discontent.
Faith plus Peace plus Love equal eternal Life.'
Wishing everyone a blessed Christmas,
The star slowly returned to the sky,
Having left on Earth its message of goodwill

Carlo Broccoli

Thieving Time

Relentless Time despoiling Life
steals earthly years away.
Entreating pleas won't change the course
not for a single day.

And in the raping, thieving Time,
oblivious to pain,
will slake his lust without remorse
and tears are all in vain.

The monster leaves his fiendish brand
on beauty and on plain,
and rich and poor, and good and bad
will all display his stain.

Try at you may to circumvent
his furtherance of crime,
to beg the villain to repent
will not discourage Time.

No pills or potions will protect
the high-born or the low.
Nowhere on Earth is sacrosanct,
no place where Time won't go.

Ron Dean

Caring

If you come to me in springtime
We will talk and plan the year,
For spring's the time for looking out
We feel there's time to share.

If summer is the time we meet
We'll admire cloudless skies,
A warm breeze comes to smooth our cheek
And peace around us lies.

Autumn will bring memories,
Spirits fall with golden leaves.
I'll try to lift those spirits
Should you ever feel the need.

In winter, next an open fire
We'll dream up days of sun,
Sip warm wine and watch the flames,
Talk of journeys done.

And should you come to me in grief,
We'll talk of things that were.
But not those useless might have beens
That bring the tears and ire.

I'd take a hand and help along
A path that's dark and bare,
With the other, hold a candle
And its tiny light we'd share.

Perhaps we'll meet again in joy
With happiness to bring.
Oh, what a meeting that will be
Autumn, summer, winter, spring.

Jan Eve

The Two Falls

The first was the fall of the rebellious angels,
    Headed by Lucifer, who became Satan or the Devil;
'Lucifer' means 'Light bearer'; Christ, the Messiah,
    The Anointed, the Son of God was and is 'The Light'.
Lucifer wanted to be the Light, he chose his will,
    Rather than be subject to the Divine Will. For this he
Was thrown out of Heaven by Michael and the good
    Angels. 'I saw Satan fall from Heaven,' said Jesus.

The second fall was that of our first parents, Adam
And Eve, who were tempted and persuaded by Satan
    To eat of the 'Tree of the Knowledge', so as to
Become like God, knowing good and evil. Thus they
    Did their own thing, instead of choosing God's will.
As a consequence, they were cast out of Eden's fair
    Garden, only to find themselves in 'Paradise Lost',
Where claw and fang, suffering and pain abide.
    But hope was on the horizon! The Divine Plan 2
Swung into action. God's word, (through whom and
    For whom 'everything and everyone' that is, has come
To be), became flesh, took on our humanity, and with it
    Our sin, its resulting suffering, and through his
Sacrifice, secured our salvation, provided we responded.
    The Word, Christ Jesus, opened for us the gates of Eden,
Once closed to sinful humanity, paradise regained.

Humanity's first 'fall' had now become their 'rising' in
    Christ, in the One, Paul says that in the end, 'All' will be
Brought under Christ and He will be brought under God,
    Who will be 'all in all'. Lucifer's fall would only lead to
His eventual elimination. He has chosen to 'rule on Earth
    (Jesus refers to Satan as the Prince of this world) rather
Then serve in Heaven. We have to choose God or Satan;
    If we choose God's will we shall eat of the 'Tree of Life'.

Kevin Kempt

Mr Dallby

Beware of the man with soft hands
And of the gentle way
Who tends to call on Sunday
And knows just what to say
The elegant Mr Dallby to be precise

Asceticism with a patience smile
Cocked-fingered when raising a cup
Napkin placed but seldom required
Selecting his words as if on trial

Mr Dallby never offers opinions
The other view is invariably his own - yet
Reads Petrarch and of Rihaku can quote a snippet
Prefers Corelli to Mozart and of Picasso, well
Precocity beyond the limit

And if the lady feigns fatigue
He'll confide of recent intrigue
Concerning those who should know better
Oh yes, he did complete a novel
To high brow of course
But he received a most complimentary letter

Does he travel - 'Not far'
'Ah'
'Only from necessity' - 'I see'

Mr Dallby watches her go to the window
He recalls the late Mrs Parsons of Tunbridge
The widow who smoked black cigarettes
So unlike solemn Maude the silver-haired spinster
Who departed with scarce a whimper

As the smiling lady appraises the street
She does not heed the carpet creak

So beware of the man with soft hands
And of the gentle way.

T Cobley

The Rain In Spain . . .

We've just had our holidays in Benidorm
A lovely place so we were told
I suppose that could have been true
If it hadn't been so wet and cold
The place that we stayed at was 3 star
Well, that was a joke in itself
You could not swing a cat in the bathroom
And the bed was attached to a shelf
We exhausted ourselves with the walking
In and out every last shop
Stopping in cafés for coffee
Waiting for rainfall to stop
Well, at least I remember my packamac
I really did look such a sight
I tried to avoid little children
In case I did give them a fright
We just couldn't wait for the weekend
To be taking our flight to go home
And next time we go on our holiday
We'll try out a visit to Rome!

Jan Wickens

My First Poem

I am sixty today
Not a very great age
My life I see as a book
As I turn every page
Pictures of my girl, my boys
Few tears, lots of joy

Now flown the nest
All alone I think
Was my house a house or was it a home?
I'm sixty today
Not a very great age
But I wish I could turn
To that very first page.

Parris Perry

Little Soldier Of The Playground

Little soldier in the playground
doing battle every day,
leader of a mighty army
the future of the world one day.
Lead them on to joyous victory
through the years that lay ahead,
from your lessons learnt in classrooms
to your dreams at night in bed.
Learn your lessons well young soldier
for the battle will be long,
gird yourself with determination
while the battle rages on.
When you finally leave the playgrounds
and your mother's heart you fill with pride,
ride on out into the future
duty and honour at your side.
And when in time you meet old soldiers
along whichever path they chose,
and you reminisce about old battles
that's when the tears of memory shows.
But without the memories little man
your life will be quite plain,
and your greatest victory is yet to come
on the road to future gain.
When you hear the final bugle
and Heaven calls you to your rest,
among the soldiers of your schooldays
all heroes of the very best.

Victor R A Day

Firefighters

The fire engine goes out the station as they get another call,
The officer shouts out, 'Hurry up lads,' I say he can't half bawl.
Through red lights they go and everyone moves to give way,
Realising when he gets to town, he's gone in a bus depot bay!
He then turns the vehicle round and hears what his mate has to say
When a voice comes through from central control, 'Will you get there
                                                 sometime today!'
They eventually get to the fire and say that was very tight,
And when they go round to the side of the engine, realise they've got no pipes.
A woman comes out the front door, looking so very calm,
And shouts out, 'Sorry lads dinner's not ready yet, afraid it's another false alarm.'

Colin H Cross

Geriatric Ward

Behind bars? Not exactly but certainly imprisoned.
The highlight of the day is visiting time;
Will they come, who will come, anybody?
Meals arrive, no appetite, no strength to reach the food.
I push the buzzer and wait, what did I want?
It takes so long I have forgotten what was so urgent,
But the bed is wet and I am uncomfortable.
Home, can I go? Will I go? Others leave,
New faces take their places but I remain.
I've been here so long I forget the month.
Days are long but sleepless nights are longer.
Will I die here or survive to move
To join another group of passengers waiting for the terminus?

Angela Edwards

Great Ryburgh School

Many children have passed through
Our village school door,
Generations of families
That will be no more.

I remember my teachers
By name just a few,
And those cold times in winter
And cold outside loo.

School's stood here for years,
The corner of our street,
A stones throw from church
And a quiet place to meet.

But now it has closed
For the very last time.
What will become to the old school in the street?
Will it be a home or a holiday retreat?

Shall we just mourn at
What others we've lost?
A railway, a foundry and shop
All to our cost.

Now this old school where sums
Were once taught,
Perhaps someone got them all wrong,
For village finished with nought.

David Howe

Patent Medicine

We never saw a doctor before NHS
A chemist, the man who'd impress,
Advised and sold us potions and pills
Cos he was the one to heal all our ills.
So at the first sign of a cough or a cold
Off to find the best, for young or old.
Milk of Magnesia and Radio Malt
But never a word about 'intake of salt'.
Castor oil, Tiger Balm and embrocation.
Parish's Chemical Food, a new innovation,
Andrew Liver Salt, a good daily dose
Taken regularly, brings relief to those
Who may find that other patent stuff
Can bring with it problems to rebuff.
Pink pills for pale people by Carter
Will help to avoid some being martyrs
To what ails them, or could Beeham Pills
Be the right answer to all their ills?
But maybe Enos, taken at night,
Is just the thing to put them right
And if, perchance, we scraped our knees
Then Germoline was sure to please.
Alas we now get our prescription
From the doctor who, hearing description
Of our ills, gives pills we cannot name!
It's really and truly just not the same!

June Burman

Argus The Album

One hundred eyed
Cave giant guardian.
Hermes Fabians pan-piped
Somnolent potion,
A lullaby of death.
Greek mythology.
Casting the dye
Of multi-faceted album.

Cut impressions -
Pioneer vinyl monster;
Cat tongue stylus
(Nine lives)
Licking revolving grooves:

A fretboard -
Brazilian Rosewood Crafted.
Space-age guitar wand.
Dexterous wizardry.
Raised goblet plectrum,
Toasting mellifluous nectar chords.
Mystical themed ensemble,
Conjuring prophetic revelation
And sunken bowl valley
Battle fury.
Hipgnosis cover artwork -
A roman centurion.
Clutching a barbed spear.
His bastion shoulders
Wine-coloured tunic draped.
Crossed to another kingdom.
Bell dome helmeted,
His visor gaze surveying
Green and yellow
Quilt patchwork landscape.
That Glastonbury-type mouth
Exuding Beltane fire incantation.
And a UFO
Crossed to another dimension.

Paul Dunne

Lest We Forget

Where have all our idols gone?
There were but scarcely few
Left from the war to end all wars
For the old red, white and blue
They gave their all to K&C
Us old-uns all remember
They fought for years to keep us free
From 39s September
In fields and sea some have remained
Their peace be everlasting
But those returned no spoils have gained
Just empty nets they're casting
Their vital years were given
To keep this country free
From tyranny and oppression
For folks like you and me
Alas we have forgotten
The brave beloved few
Although we see them often
In the DHSS queue
For war we sang their praises
In peace their worth denied
We promised high rank places
Let's face it we all lied
We've left them on the beaches
Like seaweed to decay
How cruel we are like leeches
With people's blood we play
We stole their youth and in return
We gave them little money
No dignity or right to earn
From this land of milk and honey
We hear so much of others' need
And rise to the occasion
We'd give some more I'm sure indeed
With a little more persuasion
To the OAPs as they are now
Their past worth just forgotten
Why should they have to scrape and bow
Which makes them feel so rotten?

Why can't we raise their pensions much
They gave to us when needed?
They never shrank from the Nazi touch
They never begged or pleaded
Why should they now for right to live
Their twilight days contented?
They gave so much when asked to give
To a cause that's so demented
If not for them where would we be
Now the war's long over?
Surely now it's plain to see
Not on this bed of clover
Let's change the weight of gravity
And raise our warriors high
Relinquish their depravity
Cut the bonds we tied
Give them wealth they justly earned
For the duties they all met
Strike now and see their crosses burned
Strike now lest we forget.

I J Smith

On The Quay

The long light moves across the timeless sea.
Vistas of sun and wind! Let us sail home!
There let us live, where we so yearn to be,
There let us stay, with no more wish to roam.

Our ship is waiting at the water's edge,
Weathered by the salt oceans, friend of waves.
We board the ship, and make a silent pledge
To travel to that land, that us enslaves.

The cliffs shine in the sun. Soon we will sail
This world of sea and sky, one endless blue.
How wonderful, to see our love prevail,
And to begin again a life that's true.

Patricia Marston

A Zoo Tiger Speaks

I'm fine here - OK.
Twenty-five paces take
Me all the way
Across my cage.
That's not bad, you know.
My father's cage was
Only twelve paces square - so
I've done pretty well for myself
Don't you agree?
Better than those tigers
Who are what's called *free*.
Who must be lonely and hungry
Not well fed like me.
Here the food's regular
Two o'clock every day.
Of course - it doesn't move
I dream of food that runs away.
But my food never
Tries to escape my paws.
It just lies there
Ready for my jaws,
Whenever I feel like it.
Sorry - I can't stop and talk
Any longer - I've so much to do;
Time for my afternoon walk.
Excuse me - just before I go,
I hope you don't mind me asking
Do you happen to know
What day - what year - it is?

John W A Roberts

Getting Old

I just tripped in the bedroom
'You're not safe,' my daughters said
'The next time you could break your hip
If you fall out of bed.'

Deep down I know that what they say
Is true, but nonetheless
It's hard to let a stranger
Help you wash and eat and dress.

They whisked me off to hospital,
Now I can't go home I'm told.
So my house with all its memories
Stands waiting to be sold.

My brain is just as active
But the signals don't get through
It's Parkinson's Disease they say
And some other ailments too.

At least I chose the home I'm in
The staff here are so kind,
So I just take the tablets
And pretend that I don't mind.

It's what my family wanted
My dear husband is long-gone,
But no one can take my memories
They will always linger on.

Susan Furminger

The Falling Swallow

I one evening saw a swallow fall from the sky
Is it dead? I wondered as I was about to pass it by.
I stopped and looked all around, there I saw the bird on the ground.
Is it dead? I wondered as I picked it up and wondered why
This small blue swallow had fallen from the sky.
Then a soft quiet voice spoke to me,
'Lift up its feather and see what you see.'
This I did and saw a small red spider and knew then why
This little blue swallow had fallen from the sky
The red spider on the swallow blood had fed
I knocked it off and stood on it until it was dead.
Now watching the swallow I wondered if it would fly
Or would the bird just stay in my hand and lay there and die?
Then off the swallow went up into the sky,
And then flew around and around me as if to say goodbye,
I felt good inside because it was well as far as I could see
And this small swallow was never seen again by me, or was it?
For when flying high in the sky all little blue swallows look alike.

CJ Cross

Monday Morning Early

The sun has risen slow as a mean-spirited man giving praise
The sky is a compromise of yellow and pale blue
I wait to go out, as if released from a life-sentence of responsibility
                                                    and council tax.

The streets are bleached clean of people,
Clattering like cutlery through the town and into the lazy unsure distance.
So far the new day is like a freshly washed shirt,
Free from the stains and smells of life, half-digested and thrown away
                                                    as if worthless.
But after dinner the burning sun soaks into my body and soul
And again I try to score the perfect ten and manage one,
Such is the fallibility of Man wrapped up in his flashy suit of arrogance
                                                    and discontent.

Laurence D E Calvert

The Show

The produce is here,
The tables are full,
The Judge is running around like a bull,
He looks at this one then at that
Is the fruit cake really flat?
It has to be for all the rules
State emphatically, that's the way to choose
The winner's prize
From all the rest
It really must be seen to be best.

G Mountford

Sting

So what has changed?
Still the brown hair and eyes
She grew from a child who was shy,
Into a woman as time passed by.
Independent a career aspiring,
Horizons new and a pension too
Not a little dependent daughter
But a woman unafraid of life
And what it taught her.
So how could a father misconstrue
Her very personal point of view?
For him a maid in his old age, he thought
For her a chapter she never sought.
As years rolled by and they drifted apart
Father in a fit of peak disowned
His daughter and cut her from his will.
Just for being an independent lass
He carved her out and that seems crass.

Rosemary C Whatling

21st Birthday

My 21st birthday was such an event,
we held it at Layer Marney Towers
amid Tudor splendour in the Gallery Hall
a birthday party was more like a ball.
Now I am sixty it seems far away
looking back on the event happily I say.
My father in contrast had his 21st birthday
on an aerodrome cold and bleak,
with a bottle of beer as a birthday treat.
He watched the 90 Squadron bombers leave, their fate to meet.
So happy 21st birthday Forward Press,
it shows what an achievement and what an event.
Let's hope Forward Press continues to thrive
and perhaps you will be printing when I'm 99.

Josephine Sach

The Pact

Away with it all my love
Come lay by my side
To share the final embrace
And without tears our goodbyes
Come now old girl
No panic prayers or fear for the soul
Just guests leaving quietly
When for them it's time to go.

Kevin Cobley

Untitled

His voice is still but his presence is near,
his memory remains so very dear.
His body now lies beneath the sand
of a far-off arid desert land.
His country called and he went to fight
for what he thought was just and right.

He never knew his son so small
now grown with manhood strong and tall.
He looks now just as his father was
when he gave his life for country's cause.
Although I've never wanted another
it's been quite a job being father *and* mother.

I look back on the years as I kneel to pray
in the quiet church on our son's wedding day.
I feel my dear husband's love surrounding,
as I kneel, my heart abounding with joy
for my son and his young wife
to whom he pledges his love and his life.
The same vows we made I shall always keep
until I join you my darling in your quiet sleep.

Gladys Mills

Tilbury Fort In Sonnets

When boy met girl around the town of Tilbury,
Tradition would dictate some things to do,
And if seduction's art was handled skilfully,
A summer's afternoon, 'neath sky of blue
Would see most couples hand-in-hand held walking
Along the old fort road to Tilbury Fort,
With eyes in silence, doing all the talking,
Hers full of questions, his full of retort.
And in the fort and all the grassland round it,
So many couples innocently lay
Some sought to kiss, while some sought more (and found it),
Some just held hands and dreamed the day away
And if that fort, where good Queen Bess did dwell
Could talk, it wouldn't half have some tales to tell!

The fort was a defence against the Spanish,
If their armada sailed into the Thames,
The cannons readied primed, the foe to banish,
(All Tilbury folk know these historic gems).
It gets used now for mock historic battles
But rarely more than once or twice a year
And when the warlike sound no longer rattles
The sound of nature's all there is to hear.
Yet once, the moat was full of people swimming
While others rowed in boats and looked for eels,
The whole place, full of life, was fairly brimming
With sounds of laughter and delighted squeals.
As mums sat down, the kids to watch and hear
And dads slipped in the World's End for a beer!

The fort was mine for many happy hours
I'd go, sometimes with friends, sometimes alone,
And walk the dungeon corridors and towers
Or ride a bike around the walls of stone.
Sometimes we'd hire a boat and all be sailors
Till, 'Come in number six!' our dreams would end
Or down the dungeons, prisoner and gaolers
Would battle to the fearsome gory end!

Then, as the other gender we discovered
The area became our courting ground
The mysteries of life were soon uncovered
Answers to many questions soon were found.
Six hundred years and still the fort survives
It's played a major part in many lives.

Mick Nash

A Tidy Someday

I like things to be tidy,
I like things to be neat.
When things are in straight lines
it's then I feel complete.

I like to do the cleaning
I don't do things by half.
After three hours I get sweaty
and I like to have a bath.

I like it to be spick and span
and the dinner in the frying pan.
I like to Hoover to a song
I like to feel that nothing's wrong.

I like Christmas to be sorted
and all the presents boughted,
while lying in the sun in June
you can never be too soon.

You're having a laugh you might say,
no one could work that hard all day.
You're right, I am a lazy cow,
it's just a far-off dream for now.

Julie Boitoult

The Bus Show

There's magic in the air
And the sun is shining fair,
And the crowds are everywhere,
It's the bus show of the year,
And coaches also here
People taking photographs
And bringing all the cheer.

There's magic in the air
As the buses fill the fields,
And the crowds spread everywhere,
Each hand a camera wields;
Coaches green, coaches blue
And buses, large and small,
What a feeling! What a view!
And many a filling stall.

Owners many, owners proud
Stimulate the rising crowd;
But showing off each noble bus -
And each is great to see them, thus
This spectacle of great delight
Of lesser and of greater height
Displays a great and skilful craft
Resulting from real hard graft.

There's excitement in the air
As the tour buses do fill:
For many have the flair
For revving up this thrill,
And as the bus-filled hours
So joyfully pass by,
A loud speaker announces
That judging time is nigh.

Assembling all in shiny glow
A sparkling end to this great show,
The winners all are forward brought
The treasured trophies yet to sport
A happy end to this great show,
Cheer and claps unbounded flow.
The buses, coaches, people all
And stallholders can never pal.

John Ellis

August

Ants a-swarming
Wasps a-chewing
Birds a-pecking
Flies hover
Foraging for nectar's sweetness

Buds a-forming
Peals falling
Insects mating
Apples ripen
As the warmth and rains pour down

Leaves a-fluttering
Grapes a-forming
Plums a-dropping
Laden boughs
The feast of summer's harvest.

P Homer-Wooff

Three Haikus

The sunrise wakes me
Streaky sky pink and yellow
My heart lifts in hope.

Late in the garden
Heavy scent of lavender
Brings me peaceful sleep.

A swan with cygnets
Gliding by on the water
Calms the troubled soul.

Meg Nellist

The Netherland Riddle

Mother!
Where did you hide my shadow
spiked and pricked, under the tall grass
grappled by granite, sodden in leaves
drenched in the tall grass that covered my knees?

Did you
leave it on a hook by the door
to dry out from the rain?
Mother! Did you bring it in again

from where it was buried, from
the galloping marsh and the harsh terrain
did you? - Bring it back from the
bony hood that scythes through the tall grass
where I stood?

Mother - have you cradled my shadow
in your arms - sewn time back to the youthful bed
found the cotton, found the thread?
Mother where are you in the tall grass
where my knees once stood,
to gather the shadows on this dark wood?
Has the tall grass grown over my knees
so they hide in the shade, wherever they please?

R A Toy

Winter Wood, Essex

This wood is not strange by day:
In winter's stiff embrace
The stream forgets to flow;
One robin sings alone;
And every twig and every stone
Is known and commonplace.

But night is another time
Of leaves, bright, silver-shoon;
Of spell and happenstance;
Of spider, bat and owl,
Of fox and badger's prowl,
When the hidden people come to dance
Under a pagan moon.

Pamela Constantine

Scene In Suffolk

Furrows in foreground, lying in lines,
Bluey-green background prickled with pines.
Hazy horizons clothed in cloud,
Capering children, laughing aloud.

Cottonwood cloud-ships sail 'cross the sky,
Proudly and pleasing to east man's eye.
Hay-cropping horses nuzzle and neigh
Bountiful buttercups swingle and sway.

Harrow on headland, rotting with rust,
Pheasants, like phantoms, dance in the dust.
Soft stretching shadows, ghostly and grey
Hauntingly herald the dying of day.

Bob Shelcot

Norfolk At Night

I stepped over the stile between the hedgerows
I trod on turf wet and glistening with dew,
I made my way to the field centre
My heart was with you, I knew.

I drew deep breath in exciting anticipation
And exhaling a misty sigh
I stood in the field's centre
And gazing I studied the sky.

Two million twinkling bright lanterns
I observed lit the heavens so bright,
I saw bold Mars chasing Venus
And considered their heavenly plight.

I craved for the celestial bodies
And whispered to the moonless sky
'I love you oh Venus
Let me be by your side.'

The sparks of firing starships
Flickered in the sky so deep
Their lights stimulated my passions
As I thought of you in your sleep.

The lights of brave Norwich
Flickered many miles away
And above, a spark from bright Saturn
Left a trace turning quickly to grey.

My world of bright starlight
Came slowly thus to an end
As the light of slow sunrise
Came soberly over the Fen.

Martin G Roberts

A Long Way Home

We basketed our birds on the Tuesday night
To be transported far away
For a race from Lerwick, in the Shetland Isles
The graveyard for pigeons they say.

Liberation took place early Saturday morn
With many miles of sea to cross
But to encounter fog or birds of prey
Would surely mean a loss.

The Highlands of Scotland, a welcomed sight
When flying south for home
The journey was long, but they had to keep on
To reach home, before it came night.

I saw them coming in the afternoon
But they seemed so far away
They looked like dots up in the sky
And they seemed to be coming my way.

High in the sky, the sun shone bright
With a light breeze from south west
But thoughts in my head, could it be them
Coming home from their biggest test?

As I waited and watched eyes transfixed to the sky
My excitement was hard to maintain
For the pigeons I knew, as they come into view
Wheeled from the group up high.

They dropped like stones and came in fast
Clapping their wings with glee
As if to say we have made it back home
A most wonderful moment for me.

Five hundred plus miles, on a lovely day
Is not very hard says your friend
But when you think of the miles
They have flown with great style
Makes you feel proud to be part of them.

Ray Gallagher

Alive Without Living

Born into a world of sheer deprivation
Dungeon children, from their first breath
There was to be no normalization
By an evil father denying the right
To sunshine, flowers in bloom
The changing seasons outside

A loving mother did her best
She . . . the source of their existence
Slave to the master's behest
Threats, preventing resistance

Minds cannot comprehend
That the victims yet survived
Then, facing all that's near
Questions . . . carefully contrived

Describing this father of many
Cannot be found in one word
May the anguish they endured
Be applied to him
None shall wail
It is assured.

Maria Johanna Gibbs

Beneath The Cross

(A pantoum about High Suffolk)

The orchids on Chippenhall Green,
the Waveney winding its way,
what wonderful things to be seen,
High Suffolk - a morning in May.

The Waveney winding its way,
rape, ragged, festooning the lane,
High Suffolk - a morning in May,
black barns standing proud in the rain.

Rape, ragged, festooning the lane,
already a poppy in sight,
black barns standing proud in the rain,
old churchyard as silent as night.

Already a poppy in sight,
what glory can Heaven impart!
Old churchyard as silent as night
while waiting to gladden my heart.

What glory can Heaven impart?
What wonderful things to be seen;
while waiting to gladden my heart
the orchids on Chippenhall Green.

Peter Davies

Ode To A Cyclist

No insurance, no road tax
Bikers who, with manner lax
Cycle up and down the road
Trying motorists to goad.

They peddle on with all their might
Ignoring all the traffic lights
Straight along the middle lane
Round the bend and back again

Arm extended, turning right
But who turns left with speed of light?
Round the gutter, in and out,
Pausing then to give a shout

'You motorists don't own this place
OK then, you want a race?
Just wait until I get in gear,
Then watch my dust - oh dear, oh dear!

The chain's come off, oh woe is me
No race today that's plain to see
I'll put me helmet on me head
And goad some other motorist instead!

Cars in queues at traffic lights
Oh wonderful - that gap's quite tight
I'll wobble up between those cars -
Oh sorry dear, me handlebars

Just happened then to catch your paint
It must be cos I'm feeling faint
No, sorry I don't carry cash
I can't pay you for that awful gash

You are insured? - oh well that's good
I don't like to be misunderstood
I know that you were stationary
But your car upped and leapt at me

Impaled itself upon my brake
Don't take that tone for heaven's sake!
It can't be helped, it was not me,
It must be your fault - can't you see?'

Then off they go, all three abreast
'Catch up Pearce - oh do your best!
If we link hands, then we will be
Home in time for toast and tea'

So off they go, misunderstood
In high dungeon, but feeling good
Speeding up and down the path
Oh what a day - a right good laugh!

'Tomorrow we'll try four abreast
Cos after all they've passed a test
But still they will not better me
That's what they think - but we shall see . . .'

Daphne Goddard

The 'It' Factor

We concede the point you're making Sir, and in certain case we do concur,
That would-be lechers, gropers and worse! Deserve to have their noses burst.
But speaking in a lighter vein, for ladies who let their fantasies reign.
You must allow - morale soars high, should a Clarke Gable clone give a woman the 'eye'.
Come on - be fair, you wouldn't let Sophia Loren stroke your hair!
We wager you would and nor would you tell
In fact, you'd commit decorum to Hell.

In a Harold Robbins' steamy tale, sexual harassment seems to prevail.
It happens in lifts, it happens in planes,
It takes place on mountains and also in trains.
The heroines never seem to protest and are never caught wearing a thermal vest.
Mind you, sometimes the place is small, Harold always has the gall
to wickedly think of an awkward venue
like Tesco's Home & Wear, or a Boeing's cramped loo.

Do men ever go in fear of a grope, and if they did, how would they cope?
Would they rush to the boss and the culprit indict?
Or think - this is lovely - I've no wish to fight.
Lasciviousness can be quelled with a glance
to erstwhile Don Juans who fancy their chance.
For anything more ambitious than that,
then we grant the offender should be put on the mat.

In summary then, bar an offensive maul,
surely it's better to be fancied than not to be fancied at all?

Patsy McLean

Pirates

Those rough English pirates roamed the Spanish Main,
Mad drunk on Jamaica rum, they murdered just for gain.
And sometimes for sport, they'd 'ack off a victim's 'ead!
Or make 'em walk the plank; so the 'ungry sharks were fed.
(They'll 'ang ye 'igh from the yardarm, lads, 'afore the sun be set!)
(Cos piracy in England with 'anging is always met!)

Looming up behind their victims in the Caribbean Sea
With cannons belching fire they advanced drunkenly,
All swearing and cursing, their Captain gave a shout,
'Get ready orl me 'arties to sort the buggers out!'
(They'll 'ang ye 'igh from the yardarm, lads, 'afore the sun be set!)
(Cos piracy in England with 'anging is always met!)

And after the broadsides, grappling irons came into play,
Pistols fired through the smoke across that sunny bay;
They swung aboard the galleon, with a cutlass in hand,
Killers every one of them - this vile mutinous band,
(They'll 'ang ye 'igh from the yardarm, lads, 'afore the sun be set!)
(Cos piracy in England with 'anging is always met!)

Stately Spanish galleons they'd plunder by the score;
Swiftly smashing open the door to the treasure store.
Creaking chests of treasure overflowing with coins of gold,
Knee-deep in diamonds, rubies and 'eirlooms of old.
(They'll 'ang ye 'igh from the yardarm, lads, 'afore the sun be set!)
(Cos piracy in England with 'anging is always met!)

Oh those flashing emeralds, and rubies glinting red,
What a mix of treasure for which those pirates bled.
'But will it all be worth it lads, come the end of day?'
For then the Admiralty will 'ave its legal say!
(They'll 'ang ye 'igh from the yardarm, lads, 'afore the sun be set!)
(Cos piracy in England with 'anging is always met!)

The rich lords of the Admiralty hate all pirates bold,
Haughty in their duty, red-faced above their gold.
Hanging, is their verdict; and never leniency,
They know, the rope's waiting, lads awaiting all of ye
(They'll 'ang ye 'igh from the yardarm, lads, 'afore the sun be set!)
(Cos piracy in England with 'anging is always met!)

D Taylor

More Ravings

(With apologies to EA Poe)

Sitting down in raven fashion
Feeling rather bold and dashing,
Thought I'd do some number crunching
Saw this kettle by the wall.
So I set myself a poring
On a matter bleak and boring
Like how to calculate the rating
Of that kettle by the wall.
Found that I could still recall
Joule and physics learnt at school.
Filled that kettle up with water
As my teacher said I ought to,
Measured one three quarter litres
From that jug upon the wall.
Then I timed it out to boiling,
Full five minutes it was toiling
Then I figured out the heating,
Multiplied by four point two,
Divided this by time in seconds
To give the rating, as I reckoned
Just about two kilowatt
Which I think is no bad shot
For a raven who is sure
He will labour nevermore.

M Waller

Lies

You are my love, my love you are
The fairest I have seen
Come lie beside me on my bed
Tel me where you've been.

Come let me taste the honey
I only need one sip
Come lie to me and let those lies
Come fourth from loving lips.

Come fill me full of sweet desire
And when the rush is done
Lie to me again my love
Say I'm the only one.

You are my love, my love you are
Life is but a dream
Come lie beside me on my bed
Tell me where you've been.

Beryl Shailes

Untitled

His strong arms shield me like wool
His gentle words heal my pain
His breath on my hair gentle as angels
Sweet kisses reveal his love

When young his arms held me tightly
His words of love captured my heart
His breath on my hair hot with desire
His kisses revealing his love.

Ann Bell

We Will Remember Them

The life of a soldier in the First World War,
Was not an easy one.
Mainly for the kids who ran to join up,
Expecting it to be easy and fun.

But fun was the worst word that you could use,
To describe the trauma and fear.
That ran through the veins of those soldiers,
To describe the reason they aren't here.

The squelching mud in the trenches,
The hell holes filled with rain.
These men were tools for the generals,
To send to their death over and over again.

Nothing can truly compare,
To the conditions way back then.
Nothing can ever speak,
What was felt by the dying men.

Artillery strikes and snipers,
Not a single place was safe.
From the tanks on the field,
Or from the air due to a strafe.

The war is spoken of in numbers,
Not how it should be told.
It doesn't matter if they were poor or rich,
It doesn't matter if they were young or old.

No summary can be made,
Or the army overall.
For every person should be remembered,
For they all stood their ground strong and tall.

They all fought for that they believed in,
For king and country too.
Some fought for their families,
Maybe someone related to you.

No words on paper can ever explain,
The loss of life those years.
The endless graves, the countless dead,
It brings forth from me my tears.

So the 11th of November, 1918,
Was when the armistice was signed.
It was the end of the war to end all wars,
Until nineteen thirty-nine.

'They shall not grow old as we who are left grow old
Age shall not weary them, nor the years condemn.
At the going down of the sun and in the morning
We will remember them'.

Ryan Hill

The Rose

Once there was a red rose, its petals pure and sweet,
Raindrops stood atop it, in a line, very neat.

Once there was a red rose, its scent was sweet and pure,
The thorns, very scratchy, 'twas glazed, evermore.

The rose it stood with thousands, in a field out of the way,
A melody it played one fine summer's day.

The rose was very tiny, a petal floats to the ground,
It lands so very smoothly, a tiny twinkling sound.

The rose it grew so large above the hilltops it could see,
Open more stretch, to touch the sky, to protect you and me.

The rose it planted one thorn, upon the steely ground,
Another step it took right then, it rolled over, round and round.

The roses they joined hands, to sing and dance with glee,
A whisper, shhh, we dance once more, a petal for your tea.

A tiger it came bounding, in leaps and bounds with ease.
To take the rose far, far away, the flowers it would tease.

Andréa Watson

Autumn's Golden Dawn

There is a gradual loss of identity, as late summer fades away,
New shade and colours in great wildwoods, greets a different day,
A golden stretching splendour, of bright hues in autumn's dawn,
Reminds us of the wonder, as a beautiful season is reborn.

Two bright-eyed robins, perch upon a willow's twisted stem,
Branches clothed in pearls of white, sparkle in filtering sun,
Set against an ivory mist, of early morning dew and wet,
A pair of kingfishes alight upon a bough, casting a colourful silhouette.

Red deer browsing among green flora walk through coppice side by side,
A silver fritillary butterfly, feeds on bramble, near a quiet woodland ride,
Dog violet with early morning purple orchid, bloom in soft fertile ground,
Tall conifers and pines gently sway, in harmony of silent sound.

Brent and many wildfowl, are mirrored in a red autumn sky,
Circling over mudflats, soaring in thermals they climb and fly,
A seasonal time of movement, many will leave our isles,
While others are heading towards us, traversing untold miles.

A captivating scene alive, with peaceful charms of season,
Rustic shades of the fall, is racked with rhyme and reason,
Pastel hues of nature mingle and provide camouflage for foraging birds,
Adding to scenes of exquisite beauty, which helps paint a thousand words.

Jim Wilson

School Memories

I broke my wrist, and the therapist
Asked me, among questions, what my hobbies were.
So I said, 'Where do I start?
I dabble in so many things,
Photography, antiques, maps and art
Poetry comes into mind,
Of schooldays, when we had to find,
Words that rhymed.
Spelt correctly as well,
So a dictionary on hand to tell
Of words, we knew not, at the time,
For us to put into a rhyme
Just the thing to pass the time.
Till break time.
Sometimes, we would have a spelling bee,
Sharpening pencils, would be the norm,
Sharpening brains could be, a mental ability.
To shine and spell the words, just so
Would give one a big, big glow, for the team.
Am not sure if girls did best,
All done, with added jest.
Then teacher with the board and chalk,
Would add up points, and then talk,
To say, which team had won.'

Mabel G Moore

Paradox

Shedding light
        upon black shadow,
arms uplifted,
        breasts defenceless,
show a warmth
        of understanding
of her form
        the contrasts moulding
which his hands
        delight in holding,
as his heart protects, enfolding.

Satisfying,
        undemanding,
and unfinished
        it is their loving
so that it
        remains imperfect;
they are mortal
        only lending
undiminished
        and unending,
each their selflessness defending.

In the silver
        of the faucet,
as the water
        cascades gently,
see they only
        mortal image
purifying
        in reflection.
God's own mirror
        of correction,
for He makes our soul's selection.

As in prayer
        the meditation
joins their souls,
        their heart and spirits
hot desire and
        calm refreshing,

they shall sleep
      in peaceful sharing;
each respects
      the joy of caring
each the others burden bearing.

Full-lipped passion
      bathed in moonlight,
seeks a blessing
      in the darkness;
thoughts refusing
      to keep silence,
laughing with
      the joy of weeping,
tell of harmony,
      and keeping
lips together, they lie sleeping.

Then as Dawn's light
      strokes the curtain,
(and a thrush
      outside is singing)
breaks the spell
      as they lie waking,
bodies still
      but soul's desires
fill with love
      which He inspired
and awareness which He fires.

When in grace
      at last parting
has to come,
      perhaps for ever,
though the miles
      of God's pure Heaven
separates
      their bodies yearning,
now of all times
      they are learning
that forever, love flows, burning;

and they know
     that it will never
fade and die,
     as is the custom.
This is chosen
     for their comfort.
Free yet slaves
     and never taking,
not alone
     and never breaking
hearts - but rather oneness making.

Janet Miller

Sweet Dreams

Sweet dreams are for everyone and everyone who sleeps,
Sweet dreams are little secrets that we like to share or keep.
Sweet dreams have always led us to a place where we don't know,
And sweet dreams can make up stories but with truth they sometimes show.

Sweet dreams can make us happy, or even sometimes sad,
Sweet dreams are mostly funny when they seem to be so bad.
No matter what sweet dreams you have and no matter if they're true,
For when you wake up, you're sure to find, a family that loves you.

Tracey Farthing

My Personal Thank You For Twenty-One Years

(Dedicated to the Forward Press team and all the poets old and new)

I hold my letter and give a quick glance,
Have I been given a wonderful chance?
To have a poem along with the young and old,
The story of twenty-one years to behold.

Mine has been chosen to help celebrate,
This very, very special date.
It is not the winning; it's just a perfect time,
To join with others that write in rhyme.

Soon I will have a special book,
What is in it, I cannot wait to look.
With poetry just what will people say,
To help you celebrate your big day?

My words can only come from the heart,
So that is where I will start.
Twenty-one years of anticipation,
Has gript so many, from many a nation.

The poems all varied from short and long,
Some in limericks, some in song.
The best were chosen by the Forward Press team,
I feel like the cat that got the cream.

From over the nation stories are told,
Memories of so many at a glance unfold.
Treasured, momentous, happy and sad,
Some are funny, some are nicely mad.

Dedications to so many, from far and wide,
When we see it in print we glow with pride.
No better way can our messages be conversed,
Then to send them to you in verse.

I wish you a very happy twenty-first birthday,
And a big thank you I would like to say.
For having the insight to fulfil your dream,
Putting poetry on the map to be seen.

W E D Edwards

Today

Today the river of life is blue
Colours play a part in all what we do.
For some reason the green fields of nature
Shout to us that there is a presence, greater than us.
Yellow, like sunshine, warm and bright
Black at midnight with touches of white.
Pink and red bold to wear
This is only part of the spectrum
Nothing is black or white
Grey in-between.
Orange to cheer
Purple sad
Gold and silver regal indeed
Just imagine a world without colour
What would it be like?
I'm glad to have seen
So many colours, a richness like a tapestry
There for you as a picture, captured
Seen with my eyes
No film, camera
Or a modern aid
Just a gift from birth
To us tailor made.

Rachel E Todd

Things That Count

A little word of praise
and a lovely smile,
the things that count for happiness
that make our lives worthwhile.

Don't be always finding fault
and saying unkind things,
such words we can never take back
and unhappiness it brings.

See the best in everyone
give praise where it is due,
and always do to others
what you would like done to you.

Be the good Samaritan
helping others all the time,
being loving, doing good deeds every day
and remember to be kind.

To hear those pleasant sounding words
when we say, 'Well done!'
A little word of praise
it will help in the long run.

Lindy Roberts

The Eternal Cyclist

There is a place wherein the hills roll gently ever downwards.
The sunshine always falls upon one's back,
And the breeze skips gladly behind.
Fresh meadows await a picnic, birds sing sweetly,
Beasts of field and forest go about their business unfettered,
And yet hinder not the pace of a cyclist.
Quiet resting places abound and company is good.
Streams rush by busily filling distant lakes.
Distant snow capped peaks look down benignly upon those enjoying a journey.
The peace is all encompassing and there are no cars.
In a place such as this the eternal cyclist may hope to abide.

M D Hodder

Save What's Left Of The World

Come and join us citizen, show the world that you care
Come help us in our fight, the world is not beyond repair
Help us right the wrongs, past generations have caused
The environment has suffered, so let's vote in new laws

God just did not make the world, just on behalf of Man
The plants and the wildlife were also part of His plan
He gave to Man more knowledge, but not to use it to abuse
Those less fortunate beings, whose survival we can choose

Yes, the choice has been ours, whether they lived or died
In destroying their forests they had nowhere left to hide
Killed for their furs, their feathers or their skins
Or just slaughtered for pride, one of Man's more deadly sins

We have poisoned the water, we have poisoned the air
This Earth that was so rich, is now polluted almost rare
Now Man is taking his own turn, our extinction is nigh
Millions are starving; it's our last chance to try

First of all let's find out just what harm has been done
Trace all the wildlife, that once here now are gone
Find out all the reasons, for the mistakes of the past
It's our last chance to save what's left, so let us all act fast

If we set an example then our children will see
That the cause is not hopeless, and they will want to be
Part of the new world, just as nature intended
Where Man respects the beast and the carnage is finally ended.

Don Woods

This Is The Life - It's All In Your Hands

Joined together as a blessing or in prayer
Caressing lovingly to show that you care
Clasped, entwined as two lovers meet
Soothing, stroking the kitten at your feet

This is the life - it's all in your hands

Moulding the clay as hands sculpture away
Kneading the dough for the bread each day
Fingers typing on a computer board
Hands flashing across a musical keyboard

This is the life - it's all in your hands

Planting bulbs and seeds to sow
Pruning the flowers as they grow
Selecting the fruits from trees and the vine
Rubbin' in pastry for the tart - so sublime

This is the life - it's all in your hands

Preparing the medicines to keep you well
Printing the picture you would hope to sell
Holding the racquet - serving the ball
Placing the dominoes - ready to fall
This is the life - it's all in your hands

Clasping the paintbrush or another tool
Serving the meals in the school
Sewing the garment with needle and thread
Smoothing the sheets on the clean bed

This is the life - it's all in your hands.

Gloria Ford

Feet

Sid Sen T Pede lived in the garden there
with never in the world a care,
so happy and well, right 'in the pink'
and never once of love did think.

He looked upon his home with pride;
though not so high, nor very wide,
but as he said, 'You all can see
it's big enough, there's only me.'

Then one day, following his nose,
tiptoeing on his hundred toes,
he fell in love, which made him figure
he really needed something bigger.

Somewhere with a swimming pool
- to help him keep his ardour cool -
tucked away, with trees behind
(of the floral perfumed kind).

He hoped his love would be the kind
willing to leave her ma behind;
he didn't think it very 'cool'
For Ma-in-Law to share his pool.

And though his home was now much bigger,
his future ma had a very large figure
that, with her extra million toes
would soon 'out of joint' put his nose.

'Oh Millie dear, come marry me,'
said Sid 'and then you'll surely see
that in this world so big and wide
no centipede will have more pride.'

'Well', Millie said, 'I'll have to think,
can we have our bedroom pink?
And just to prove you really care,
can I bring all my slippers there?'

Well, Sid in love was feeling kind,
'Of course, don't leave all those behind
and bring those boots for when it's cool
and 'jellies' for the swimming pool.'

Now, though Sid's house was so much bigger
he hadn't really stopped to figure
what the smell, of an extra million toes
would do to his long suffering nose.

'Millie Pede,' he said, 'now hark to me,
I think it's very plain to see,
your love of shoes is far too wide,
you'll have to learn to curb your pride.

I love you yes, but don't you think
a million pairs of boots in pink
are just too much, or don't you care
that there's no room for me left there?'

Well Millie Pede was not unkind
and didn't want to leave behind her Sid,
who really was quite 'cool'
(or do without that swimming pool),

So, though she'd like the cupboards bigger
she thought that, with her swelling figure,
(from the expected billion toes)
for now she'd best 'keep clean' her nose

And so she said to Sid, 'Ah me,
the sense of what you say I see,
I'm growing now so very wide
that though the end will give you pride

It's really best I stop and think,
of all the future bootees pink,
or blue ones, I don't really care
but space will sure be needed there.'

Now Sid was not the family kind
and thoughts of all he'd left behind,
his little home so nice and cool,
(Much better than that big wet pool)

And in this house, though so much bigger
he felt so cramped, why, he didn't quite figure,
but, crowded with several more million toes
well, just the thought of it got up his nose!

There'll really be no room for me,
my future's bleak, it's clear to see!
I'm giving up this land so wide,

for peace and comfort, blow the pride!

And Millie Pede and Ma, I think,
will likely paint the whole house pink!
To be quite honest, I don't care,
cos I just won't be living there.'

So, off he went, right then and there
and tootled off without a care,
though sometimes, something coloured pink
might make him pause a while and think.

Did he miss Millie? Did he feel pride
in all his progeny far and wide?
If he a pink dressed Pede did see,
did he think, 'she looks just like me'?

Or did he turn up his smell free nose,
sniff and say, far too many toes!
Now you are wondering this I figure,
did Millie Pede's family get any bigger?

Well, last I heard, she owned a pool
of typists, who are quick and cool
(with toes in rows, front and behind)
at typing things of every kind.

G V Lewis

When Will They Learn?

It is said that time's a healer
And the pain will slowly disappear
Of the love ones who have died in war
Oh how they paid so dear.

Sadly many hearts were broken
So many never came back
How they all fought so bravely
There was John and Ted and Jack.

Today we all paid tribute
To our most glorious dead
The people in church paying homage
Knowing many prayers were said.

The churches were full
Many came from afar
Some came there on foot
Many came in their car.

They wanted to be there
In fellowship and love
To give thanks for our brave men
To thank God above.

But sadly war it still rages
Will they never learn?
Why must man kill his brother,
Is it power and greed that they yearn?

Please get some sense those in power
They must not have died in vain
For the ball is in your court
To bring world peace again.

Doreen Spires

Don't Break My Heart

You have captured my heart
I'm taking a chance on you
I'm thinking of you when we are apart
Please don't make me blue
I'm not playing a game
I need you ever so much
I hope you feel the same
I need to feel your touch
Don't be the one to break my heart
Now these feelings have begun
Love grows at the very start
You mean the world to me
I love to have you near
You I love to see now and every year.

P Green

On My Jack Jones

It's time to untie the apron strings, 21.
Saying goodbye is the hardest thing.
I love my family, four brothers you see,
But bedsit with husband isn't too far.
Brother's home, to share with his family,
Carrying on work, seven till seven,
She's still got a flat stomach, cheeky rascals,
Leaving for job, near a home paid off,
Being ignorant to maternity, too soon to tell,
New boss at time cards, didn't you know,
Well first anniversary, little nobby arrived
Tenth anniversary, four more nobbies arrived,
Daddy's wishes all carried out, mummy's
No drinking, no smoking, no talking
To a young lady till right one comes along,
So six wonderful grandchildren arrived,
Seventy-five both now, my only wish now
Is to buy a childhood pedal scooter,
Haversack and tent, and have a holiday on my Jack Jones
Come on mums, let's go!

M Clark

The Star

I saw a star of brilliant light
travelling fast across the night,
I did not ask why it was there
it was a secret none could share.
I travelled with this star at first
across the infinite endless universe,
the fantastic colours that I saw
made me so small and full of awe.
I saw the Earth in different hues
encircled, protected in a halo of blue,
I reached out to touch this globe
as I went quickly by
but Earth was out of reach
and soft tears did I cry.
I travelled past many planets,
way past the realms of dreams,
I travelled through the darkness
to the sun's brilliant beams.
I saw the browns and greens of Earth
and flowers being born,
then sunrise brushed the sky
as I awoke that early morn.

Sylvia Partridge

A Soldier's Request

Please don't leave me here among the dirt, darkness and death
Please not here where I drew my last painful breath
Take me away from this land without water
From this place of endless pointless slaughter
A host of flapping shapes silently descend
No! Not for my leaking wounds to attend
They strut and circle in their awful haste
To be the first my cooling flesh to taste
I see no pity in their bloodshot eyes
Now they flap; dismiss the myriad flies
Wait! Something parts the squabbling horde
Perhaps a saint with flashing sword?
Comes someone to compound my grief
A wicked stony-faced body thief
Too late! All my life force's gone
Left, my bones bleaching in the sun
I hover above the bloody ground
And softly note a beautiful sound
A multitude of tongues speaking as one
The fallen arisen to deride what's been done
No limbless or contorted bodies here
No broken faces set stark with fear
Oh! And there my once departed mate
Smiling, chatting dispersed of hate
Never let this wonderful feeling cease
Yes! Do leave me here. I'm at my peace.
Oh Earth Mother! I fulfilled my mission
To fight and die for some damn politician
Who, with barely a misted eye and jaw set proud
Quickly reads my name to the honourable crowd
Then a sip of water from an ice-cold beaker
A nod and a glance; 'Thank you Mr Speaker.'

J W Coyne

Michael Jackson - The King Of Pop

Michael Jackson the king of pop,
sung and danced his way to the top.
His albums and videos are there to see,
making him the biggest star in *HisTory*.

'Thriller', 'Bad' and 'Off the Wall'
are the greatest albums of them all.
With sales up in the millions for each
the likes of which no one could now reach.

His moonwalk across the open stage,
dazzled fans of every age.
With fans cheering his every move,
Jackson was always in the groove.

The lives you've touched with your inspiration,
has given us all great imagination.
From singing, dancing and writing too,
whatever it is we can do it because of you.

You're lying now in peace and tranquillity,
forever now and all eternity.
The fan's love for you will never cease,
so please Michael, now rest in peace.

(29th August 1958 - 25th June 2009)

Andrew J Doyle

Pardon?

I know that my hearing's not perfect
I've no doubt over that
But I can hear a pin drop
And hear a baby cry
But I cannot hear my husband
When he said 'I do.'
So how did I become married
As he whispers his words of advice
But never says anything twice
But though my hearing's not perfect
I hear what I want
When I want
Then, those who speak on the telly
Those who mutter aside
And their accents are very clear
So I'm certain it's not my hearing
That is failing over the years
It's everyone else who mutters
But don't like being told.

Elaine Day

Death Of Democracy

CCTV is now all the rage,
And the age '1984' has come of age.
For silent spies all over the land,
Now have all our details on hand.
Civil liberties are a dying breed
For 'Big Brother' is now the growing creed.
And democracy is a thing of the past
As Orwell's '1984' forecast!
That only the few will have the say,
On how we are to live day-by-day.
But only until they decide we are to die
And we won't even question, 'Why?'

Derek Barnaby

Feed The Birds

The picture in the cookery book 'looked good enough to eat'
Yes, I thought, *I'll make it for a treat!*
To serve four, no cooking, well, that suited me
Just crumble biscuits, mix with melted butter
Press into it, sweeten then leave to set.
Now for the good part, add raspberries with thick whipped cream
Leave in the fridge till firm
Then on the table.
What a surprise!
No one would eat it - they don't like sweet things
The cat and dog turned up their nose
Only to be expected I suppose.
So out into the garden, throw it on to the lawn
Where birds had been waiting to be fed since dawn
What a feast they did have, not a crumb did they leave
I counted 23! Seems hard to believe
They must have thought it was their lucky day
Not often does such luxury come their way
The moral is - I must be dim
It seems an expensive way to slim!

Olive Willingale

Dobbin

Billy Brown was our milkman, old Dobbin his horse pulled the cart
Sometimes he'd get the bit in his teeth and then he just wouldn't start
Billy would holler, 'Come on boy,' but Dobbin refused to proceed
He'd stand there as stubborn as can be, a bit of a problem indeed

In the cobbled street outside my granny's, he took it into his head
He decided he wouldn't go anywhere, he didn't care what Billy said
In the commotion kids gathered round to see what it was all about
Billy was getting frustrated and then all the neighbours came out

My granny a very nimble lady came dashing out her front door
Rolling something from hand to hand, she created quite a furore
She lifted old Dobbin's tail up and slapped something on his backside
She hardly had time to put his tail down; he took Billy Brown for a ride

Red Rum could not have caught him, just like he was shot from a gun
Poor old Billy was almost horizontal, as they galloped off into the sun
Everyone roared with laugher, Granny sniggered and nodded her head
'With a hot potato stuck up his backside, he soon got a move on,' she said.

Jim Bryans

Lucky This Time

Plenty of time to get there, says the old clock in the hall.
I can even read the paper and make a telephone call!

My appointment's in an hour and I've waited very long.
For this chance to get an interview, high hopes, I'm feeling strong.

I know I'm what they're seeking, the right man for the job.
In two hours time, I'll be in work and not an idle yob!

I'd better check I'm ready, put on my watch and tie.
Oh gosh, it's nearly quarter-to, I'll really have to fly!

I haven't time to worry and think about my fate.
I haven't time to get worked-up or fidget while I wait.

I made it by hair's breadth; the job is mine and all.
So, for that, I will reprieve the old clock in the hall!

Fredrick West

Two Cats And One Dead Mouse

Looking after my friend's cat Smudge while she was away
And went into see him three to four times a day.
I made sure he had fresh water, biscuits and meat
And in return he loved all around my feet.
On the last day as I entered the house
Upon the kitchen floor lay a dead mouse.
Smudge came running up to me as much as to say
Hey, I brought you a present on your last day.
I made a fuss and gave him his fresh water and meat
I have grown very fond of him, he is so very sweet.
Then another cat appeared and I was seeing double
And thought I was having some kid of eye trouble.
For a Monday morning I was having so much fun
Just fed the other cat in case I fed the wrong one!
It is now pouring down outside so I am stuck in the house
Myself and two cats and one dead mouse.

Linda Hunt

Road Works (2) - 2008

I am a Stop/Go swinger
On a bridle carriageway,
When lights would make you linger
I stand and hold my sway.
On 'Go' when cars leap forward
I swing the other way!
There's nothing like the slowcoach
To hinder all the flow,
Before he's even started
I've changed from 'Stop' to 'Go'.
As traffic's now much lighter
I've turned the auto on,
To red, green and amber
And sod the lot who come!

Reg Anderson

Black Cat

A dark shadow appears
from the garden shrubbery.
And as it gets near I see
it is a black cat, without love.

Bedraggled and so very thin,
it's coat all matted and rough.
My heart goes out to him,
this poor black cat, without love.

I gathered him in my arms,
and took him to the hearth.
To warm his thin cold body
and cuddled him, with love.

He purred a lovely 'thank you',
and I knew we shared a moment of trust
and understanding, from a black cat,
who had found love.

Daphne I Dawkins

Parts Of The Year

October days when leaves start to fade,
Shorter days,
Colder nights,
Whiteflies in their millions cover the winter greens,
Clear sky,
Not a cloud in sight,
Lightning at night with thunder rattling the sky,
Snow moving down from the north, so the weathermen say,
Plenty of rain brings this month to a close.

February came in two thousand and nine with a coat of snow,
Temperatures of minus six,
Traffic on the road going slow,
Trains and aeroplanes grounded,
Schools closed,
Children playing in the snow,
Making the most of their time at home.
Rain flowing down the drain,
Helping to wash the snow away,
Grass left a richer green,
Rain in globules on a hawthorn tree,
The sky above all grey and dull,
Awaiting the next lot of snow.
Above the treetops a darken sky.

March what a start with lighter mornings,
The lenten lily and many others flowers in full bloom.

G F Snook

Twenty-One Today

If you want the very best to send your verses too
Pick the warm familiar place which feels a friend to you
In your palm you hold the pages you had written down
Covered with big shiny envelope, taken through the town.
A verse one million poets have been asked to write
No simple task, *hip hip hooray*
That is for lesser mortals but we are twenty-one today.
If we were to whisper, folk in China wouldn't know we're twenty-one today
The poetry books are a series of lovely showcases
So if you're chosen it would mean you are one of the best.
The British Library, Bodian Library, Oxford University Library
Library of Trimby, Dublin and National Library of Wales
Where a poet dreams, but doesn't get there by schemes.
So now you see why I carried my packet tightly through
In answer to Forward Press' request, *hip hip hooray.*
The firm who opened the gates so wide, so we could put our verse inside
To a title they can use no more, as it is only today
They are able to say, we are twenty-one today, *hip hip hooray!*

Barbara I Goode

The Snail

The petty pace of the snail is without bounds
Devoid of destination and without sounds.
Indistinguishable movement makes progress so slow,
With home on back and nowhere to go.
Nestling in the undergrowth or stuck to a spade,
There's always a snail wherever it's laid.
Stuck hard and fast which is 'true grit'
No room for time, but just to sit.
The pace of the snail is definitely slow
To win in the race for certain you know.
The snail has to conquer a soggy terrain
Whatever the weather is surely its aim.
But to admire the scenery in the garden is best
Amongst dandelions and daisies and all types of pest.
So the life of the snail you can be sure
Is peaceful and calm so who could want more?

Christine Flowers

We The Archers

We all must archers be now; being taught to
strain ourselves to a point,
aiming for a centre and avoiding the willowy fringes,
being mindful that a shower
of arrows can't be right.

To be better, takes practice
and the measure of ourselves must be counted and tallied.

But when archers of old struck targets,
did they think they were going forward
or did they feel their stillness in a field?

Alex Townsend

The River Gipping At The Maltings

Here was one of Nature's gifts.
A source of food and a sight of quiet beauty, draining the land.
Lazy meanders through High Canadas of trees,
Kingfisher dived, spider's web caught the breeze.
Long-legged wader fed on fish to his fill.
Close your eyes just a minute. Can you picture it still?
King salmon bred, leapt high in the sun.
Brown bear feasted fat on pickerel's run.

And the living water flowed.

We came to the river: used; misused; abused.
Careless days, careless ways, too much to lose.
On once grassy banks Roman legions have camped.
Enough water to float saw the Viking long boat
With trade came to the barge, the lock and the weir
To give greater depth large cargoes to steer.
Industrial Revolution brought train and engine.
The need for the barge was suddenly gone. Dereliction.

But the water still flowed.

Industrialisation. A sewer not a river.
A tidewell of filth. A taker not giver
Of food nor of pleasure to all who passed by.
Who questioned? Who answered? Who dared to ask: 'Why?'
River, lock, bank, abandoned, no longer needed.
Voices now raised, are they really all heeded?
The Coke can, the plastic, the trolley shopping,
Mar the once-was beauty of the River Gipping.

And the water?

Cliff Painter

Stowmarket Town Centre On A Winter's Day

What can you see on a snow blown day
With wind in your eyes and the sky sullen grey?

Estate agents: seven; Bankers: six; Charity shops: six;
Building Societies: four; Newsagents: three; Places to worship: no place to pee.
Video hire, Solicitor, Chemist.
Optician, Shoe shop, Florist, Taxi, TV.
Bookmaker, Takeaway, Public house, Club, a Discotheque.
Was there ever a place where lovers met?

Vacant premises: a dozen plus.
Traders to fill them? Sadly no rush.

Is there anything there to lift or inspire?
St Peter and Mary's new church spire.

More they may be. Possibly less. Some others. Who can say?
But who is counting, in Stowmarket, on a cold winter's day?

Rajni Usha Patel

In It With Me

Suffering
Thinks it's 1974
And she's waiting for a bus
Sat in the chair
At the Home
Hardly there
Skin and bone.

'I let the dog out,' she says.
'When I came back from shopping.'
But there's no dog
And no shopping
A light twinkling in her mind
One light left on
In the house that is my mother.

'Where are you, God?' I cry.
'I'm losing her by inches. Why?'
Just one reply.
He's in it with me.

The man on the tree
Suffering.

Sheila Jacobs

White Wallaby

At fifteen months she crouched feeding,
nibbling as if at waybread by the path,
stock still when she saw that they had seen her,
pure white from head to toe against the dry old green

scobberlotching in the half-light where strips of
eucalyptus bark mirrored the soft light of her eyes:
swamp wallaby, wallabia bicolor, but albino here
rarer than crows' teeth (on the Island Bend

by the Kosciuszko border) where the two field-workers,
Bellamy and Moberget, had happened to backpack by.
'Healthy stance, good coat and skin,' they whispered
as they clicked the shutter several times

shaken by the rarity of being there, at the right time
but with a camera fully charged, a beast that ate so quietly.
A snowman in the bush, they said, a cuddly toy
that shuffled, looked, and stooped again, eyeing them

until they wondered, finding her alone, how she knew
that they were safe, and whether enforced loneliness had
made her tame, how she came to fend so quietly for herself,
and whether there had been a tribe that turned her out.

Hilary Elfick

Camera Eyes

Sometimes
I don't want to distance myself
With the lens
To hide behind the viewfinder
To narrow my vision
Of family and friends

But then sometimes
I want to capture the feelings
With the light
To store the memory
To see again the moment
Of when things were so right.

Andrew Fisher

Death Of A Sibling; Unknown

I knew nothing of you until too late,
Too late to hold a tiny hand,
Too late; too little; so little.
How unfair, that when I knew,
You had long passed me by,
But a part that is me, was you,
And a part that was you, is me.

K W Hainsby

God's Winged Serpent Unwound

Centred light of ill fated stars
dense realms of spiralling fire
lodestones follow weightless - vast
with magnetic force each conspires.

A dart of flame punctures Earth's crust
God shakes the pain of contact from His fist
in symmetry formed from celestial dust
blackhole eyes, solarsoul, wounds unkissed.

The creatures roam as he sleeps
with closed eyes the angels speak;
'Evil is more ancient than you
your flesh is shadow they peer through -

drink your blood from bone cups they'll make
pound your flesh into bricks to bake
know Devil you were once of God
that Man has been spared the rod -

you fell to this new Earth by choice
when the clay was still fresh and moist
lamenting will only break your heart
hankering is a long endless path'

Night duly gave way to day
mother's creatures withdrawing
upon Earth, the open grave
he hears them weeping, crawling

It's then his sorrow, stirs to tears
and shadows seep into his pores
so God's voice of reason disappears
His voice spilt from scorched flesh and claws;

'My pain shall be felt in their hearts
and my brothers they shall become
and through them no light shall pass
our needs shall blot out the sun -

for though angels speak in dreams
with words that boil my blood in hate
upon faith naïve mankind leans
I shall teach them that it's too late -

The flesh of Your creatures is so weak
I've torn many with but a touch
with a strong spirit or so they speak
with little work this too corrupts -

lost children hungry for a master
simple beggars of belief
worshipping flesh is by far faster
for pleasure is pain's relief -

the great civilizations have passed
when they drew blood in ritual fear
like footprints in the sand never last
now I'm painting caves with useless tears -

still upon every breath I take
a million cut their own flesh
their blood pools in my mind a lake
and my strength is invigorated afresh -

in fits of anger - just for fun
I will them to leap from cliffs
to hang themselves or suck on shotguns
such suffering gives me a little lift!'

As the Devil staunches his bitter tears
thinking, *I've been among the weak too long*
a few deep breaths and his mind clears
reminding him of where he belongs

His eyes echo wide and black
no light dares to escape them
the wings that span his back
overshadow the tallest of men

Cramped by his crawlspace
flexing his muscles a dusty moth
in equal and delicate grace
with broad slow beats is born aloft

Spiralling above his smouldering domain
the impact zone that tilted the Earth
rich forest reborn desert terrain
for miles around cries nature's aborted birth

His destination led by love's memories
setting wing he idly gazes down
Man's cities encircle their cemeteries

serpent rivers hug them shitty and brown

Be it hill or valley of sickly green
bespeckled with industrious little dots
in passing he wills a few into the stream
and maybe half a dozen die in their cots

On he presses above the stolen land
with flags all a-flutter
over canyons and mountains so grand
free of creatural clutter

Once more the valleys of desolation give way
to an expanse of lights that gambol and scream
where lost souls trapped in a fruitless dream play
and life in its many sufferings teem

Both laughter and sobs rose to the Devil's ears
Man drowning their sorrows - he tuttingly thought
in the city of the golden calf full of steers
lassoed by the one-armed bandit like cattle bought

The ring-kerching of the coins rang while
he let rip a flaming arc of piss
papers reported the meteor's tail stretched at least a mile
that aside from superficial burns further showers maybe a risk

So past the paradise of the lost
his spirits as buoyant as the milky clouds
as dawn rose clearing the night's frost
now above farmland, far from the city's crowds

Fattened by the livestock of Man over time
in the habit of travelling short distances at night
mainly to take away fresh flesh to dine
cursing his complacency his chest grew tight

With muscles in knots he begins to tire
and unwinds his height to set down
his thirst as dry as a desert on fire
for refreshment blood must be found

So spotting a small farm he made it his aim
a man sat in the field on a horsedrawn plough
hitting target between two silos of grain
landing breaking the back of a sunbathing sow

The shrieks of his prey he soon stifled
but alas the farmer heard and drew near

peering round the silo narrow-eyed with cocked rifle
the sight that met him filled his heart with fear

Raising a shaking weapon swallowing back his bile
as he watched his pig being devoured before his eyes
the Devil placing the bones in a neat pile
having finished he washed it down with a handful of flies

Smacking his lips and patting his belly he turned
smiling down at the man and his raised barrel
with a satisfied burp that left the man slightly burned
lowering his aim the smoking man started to babble;

'My God that was my prize pig you filthy beast
Eve will never believe this tale from my mouth
that down from Heaven and up from Hell to feast
a demon-slaughtered Jezebel - I sorely doubt'

The last whisps of smoke coiled from his singed hair
his loss overcome he regains his composure
the hate and awe vied for control of his stare
his pallid flesh by shades grew rosier

His wide eyes once more narrowed with recognition
'Satan' was the word spat - his life, he'd bet on
At this the Devil bowed - politeness conditioned
they sat in the dust laying claw down and weapon

Nonchalance crept and gathered the farmer's face
and a woman's humming floated upon the breeze
'Oh Adam how I delight in and hate your race,'
said the Devil as he brushed away a few bees

'Likewise - alas my name is not Adam, it's Steven
On one of God's glorious days I didn't expect yourself'
'All men are one,' he replied, 'be it believers or heathens
I have a journey to make and pig meat makes me belch

Is that Eve I hear? How does she bade
To be sure it was her who tempted me
When a serpent of me, God-made
As she danced naked around life's tree'

'Vile Devil your lust precedes you
Can you not see how Man evolved?'
'Yes dear Adam I have too
through violence and greed you have become bold -

Casting shadows in the light of God

how grand your cunning mind swells
as you roll in the dirt of Eden's bog
from his favour like brothers we fell -

Your memory of me lays in myth
stories of monsters, angels and ghosts
believing at its centre blessed Man sits
that above all our Father loves you the most -

If not for me you would not exist
for I am the catalyst to all you've become
with the fruit of knowledge, your mind kissed
bonds of ignorant servitude lay undone -

ask yourself why God did not stop me
was He weary of His mindless toys?
for those who do not question are not free
so to create something must be destroyed'

'From the hind of a beast your words drop
must you relieve your rancour in my face?
Not satisfied with curdling the dream of Heaven's plot
you in turn wish to preach your b*****d faith -

Wretched Devil you will not tempt again
do not pretend you opened my eyes to the light
being separate from God is the sole suffering of men
against evil with God's blessing we shall fight;'

'You wage your wars in God's name
but what kind of name is God?
My dear Adam you must feel ashamed
for His true name you have surely forgot -

And you fight this war against evil
as their children die you belt out your song
in the ruins erect your ivory steeple
and you believe your faith is strong?

So you feed God's children to Death's maw
under perfect Heaven, why is this so?
The expression of hate is love's minor flaw
in the afterglow of battle true life grows -

With bloody teeth drawn you gnash
great Christian show me the other cheek
your love for the Lord is but a pash
a hungry wolf dressed up as a sheep'

'Foul failed angel wash out your throat
we defend ourselves from your dark nations
we are the chosen people as it is wrote
the good war has gone on for generations -

Your forked tongue licks the flavour from your words
and I've grown hungry having eaten all you've said
now I must leave to shoot those damn blackbirds
that eat the corn on which my family are fed'

Shaking his head in sullen wonder
over what Man has become
his wings beat a crack of thunder
then swept into the glaring sun

He willed a shot to go wide
and Adam winged his rotund Eve
the bullet ricocheted into a hive
and she was stung to death by bees

So humming 'Onward Christian Soldiers'
all his thoughts in a distant tree
the sole reason for the love of his labours
God's only creation that understands his needs

Shadows stretched as the disc climbed
its rays glinted catching the Devil's eye
from a gold cross then its bell chimed
one of Man's spires he had spied

This set his thoughts upon a different track
they found themselves upon a small hill
Jesus nailed - slow breathing - with a broken back
His beaten body at first glance deathly still

Prodding His side with a tinder dry stick
His olive skin crisped to a sunworn black
a voice as thin as His pain was thick
sandy lids of eyes opened just a crack

'Oh Father, what sight have You sent Me?
As I live my last on this barren Earth
if this is the Devil that You set free
then what is the pain of My suffering worth?

My father who art in Heaven
blessed be Thy immortal name
who for Man's sins shall bring Armageddon

to cleanse those hearts untouched by shame -

fearless Devil what business or mischief brings
you to this godforsaken holiest of lands
have you come to gloat over the King of Kings
hung up to die to watch my bones turn to sand?'

'Adam I have come for angels directed me so
You are one in a long line of the suffering good
in studying ancient philosophies in order to grow
so please listen and let Your pain be understood -

When I fell to this Earth buried deep in its heart
my fury beating - boiling its very core
I vowed every creature I'd tear apart
with oceans of blood washing bones upon the shore -

This seething hatred's festering energy
span its web from inside out
through its destructive force Man found Man his enemy
filling them with suspicion - greed and doubt -

Taking elements of Earth they forged weapons
with a keenness they honed the methods to kill
even though in their hearts true life beckoned
the taste of power ruled their will -

We have played our roles and paid the price
my kin guided us through our darkest hour
we bare the yoke of our necessary sacrifice
we are but plucked petals from a dying flower -

We share a direct connection with our Lord
and You fell foul at the hands of brutal men
I bow at Your feet laying down my sword
but I fear this broken world may never mend'

'Devil what of My wife and My children?
I do not fear My death but theirs?'
'Jesus knows giving life has already killed them
from their bright eyes death patiently stares -

You are the Son of God - but a man no less
with a depth of heart and insight few have attained
a teacher carrying the torch of wisdom through the darkness
Your pupils fear the fire's light and fear its loss the same -

Although You will surely die upon this day
and You shall embark upon Your journey back home

as You have - others will find the light to guide the way
to turn around the hearts on its static spinning stone'

'Fallen angel - I respect your honour in kind
for I know all is good therefore you are too
in my visions I have seen a lamb lead wolves that are blind
to survive - soil must be overturned to plant the new'

The last word fell from His cracked lips
and His life passed upon the wind
placing the memory back where it sadly sits
as He flew the tears in His eyes stinged

On our archsaviour swims the air
scanning the horizon for signs of snow and ice
a sure sign of her mirrored lair
home of love for which his holy seat sacrificed

Like swan upon water sets down
in the frozen wastes a bare tree sits
a vast black root twisting up from the ground
untouched by Man's fickle conflicts

Met by two angels without freedom
courtiers at Death's every beckon call
for our visitor caught and flayed them
promising death raises those who fall

So Death brought an end to their needs
'pon their backs open wounds - now dewinged
meat rindless - glistening oozes and bleeds
forelegs cut down they walk upon knees

Escorted to the tree of death
smiling down at the trials of blood-pulped snow
their backs broken and with laboured breath
misted from a cut mouth and a hole nose

Upon reaching the foot of the tree
the pained angels of gore lay down
with twisted non faces set with glee
heaping snow over themselves - relief found

A silhouette upon a lower branch sat
a child - her legs gently swinging
reaching out he placed a claw upon her back
with burning tears - his eyes stinging

Finding his perch beside her

with wing and arm they embrace
and his warmth grew inside her
kissing her cold hands and face

The sweetest child carved from one bone
all too lifelike in imitation
but with senses more useless then stone
a picture of still life recreation

Legs unrocking - motionless she now stares ahead
the setting sun on the horizon broke
a naked statue wrapped in a wing of red
in silence the fallen angel and Death spoke;

'Noble Devil your tears are mislaid
my sorrows reap the tears of others
as they kneel over their loved one's graves
so still your trembling heart my lover -

I am glad you have at last returned
or at least my great sadness is less
this numbing solitude has long burned
in the hollow chambers of my breast -

Tell me how long has it been my sweet?
for I am blind to this world's seasons
for I have not moved from this seat
without your warmth I found no reason'

'Oh fair and fragrant Death
I cannot help these tears I cry
for you I draw my breath
and for you all flesh will die -

Know time is only a shadow cast
sometimes it is short or long
we wait for it to pass
then wonder where the light has gone -

I smell you in the sweat of Man
as they toil ceaselessly in fields
they plant their seed in your hands
from your flesh their cities build'

'Dear Devil I know this little girl you flatter
with words of comfort as I gaze into the abyss
its true moments in eternity do not matter
for each one is as transient as a farewell kiss -

Although blind to this world I still dream
of dense woods, thick snakes, hanging - writhing
dragging a fruit sack - for help I scream
each snake bites then drops groundward dying -

I wake just short of gaining meaning
asking the multitude of souls as they pass me
but they are convinced they are dreaming
feigning ignorance as they melt into my tree -

I know not what these visions mean
consuming my thoughts since you went away
tell me grand ochre angel do you dream?
What do the thoughts of your heart say?'

'My lady, angels are my demons
I close my eyes all I see is black
they sing to me though I can't see them
open my eyes and in Hell I'm back -

The wise Lord whether in blessing or bane
rendered the company of my moon's eye closed
to see the playground of Eden's beauty again
I chose this Hell upon me He imposed -

Your dreams are an ancient collection
born from your sister life's struggle
though every tear of blood seeks direction
Man finds his peace in God's puzzle -

As each soul is bound to this tree
baring burden's greater for losing their lives
mere reflections alas dreams set free
forever life is sown and so on death thrives'

'You speak of God without a note of scorn
sweet angel of death how you have mellowed
bloody screams for revenge have become yawns
is it I who has punctured your bellows?'

'Abundant Death, my life was changed by you
the raging flames of my past now doused
and up from the ashes a phoenix flew
with tendered heart - at your feet now bows -

Imprisoned as we are in this buckled orb
with the warped flesh of Man and beast our prey
politics of Heaven remain self-absorbed

for I know not to God but to us Man prays'

'So in saying that my ever faithful Devil
your machinery runs on without its maker
and in each other we can remain to revel
because self-destructions built into human nature -

Born into illusion and driven to distraction
taught to love through the torture of fear
binds tighten with generational contractions
however far they reach - they all end up here -

Either sheep in the shadow or beasts of war
and they shall disappear under the coming tide
surely against the will of God, Man is now yours
your duty complete - rest your wings with pride -

Shed no more tears for we need never be apart
wrap me in the fire of your violent love
I shall whisper my dreams against your heart
under the silver-eyed moon and sunsets of blood'

'Blackest Death, like fallen blossom upon
a freshly dug grave as do your words sit
like blood-soaked feathers of angels dead and gone
I speak from the flames my love for you lit -

I've grown weary of Man - just the very sight
I forgot the joy of feeling your cold bones
as you say our slaves shall carry on the fight
these desolate wastes of ice reflect my home -

I have no need to return to my molten crater
for all I know Man has made it an ear to the stars
to sit by your side there is no need greater
for it reminds me of the tree we left on Mars'

The root leapt with snakes of flame
as the cogged wheels of heaven doggedly spun
innocent creations of God that Man blames
once more - through love - became one.

Ben Keats

Lonely Farmer

I see him on the brow
A lonely farmer at his plough
Silhouetted against the evening sky
His faithful dog trotting by
One horse white, the other brown
As he tills up and down
Seagulls circling in his wake
A tasty morsel for to take
In old slouch hat and hobnail boots
While in the distance an owl hoots
Bracered trousers tied with string
I know he wears a plain gold ring
He is my man, I am watching there
As he tills with loving care
We both now are grown old
Our farm soon to be sold
Machinery will take his place
And till the land at greater pace.

D Carr

Autumn Advance

It is late summer, and the sky is blue
And full of fluffy white clouds tinged with grey
Leaves on trees are turning another hue
Small creatures preparing for the affray
Of old autumn's barrage of gust and rain.
But September holds magic all its own
That haunts the memory like a refrain
It can make you sad, or maybe just prone
To regret; thinking of things unachieved
Or lost; thoughts may dwell on things so tragic
You may rise from bed feeling somewhat peeved.
If so, just think of late summer magic.

As the summer wanes, let autumn reckon
To bring fresh hope and new love to beckon.

Valerie Hall

Just One Night

Tonight in your arms
I'm wishing I could stay
And when tomorrow comes
Say you'll not be the one to stray
So far away from my heart

Tonight if those stars
Were mine to give
I'd give them all to you
For more than
Just one night with you

And when tomorrow comes
Everywhere you go
I'll be wishing I was
There with you

Tonight if those stars
Were mine to give
I'd give them all to you
For more than
Just one night with you.

K Lake

The Bread Of Life

Break thou 'the bread of life', dear Lord to me
As Thou didst break the loaves beside the sea.
And as we sing those same words so bright
May we all have our Lord Jesus in our sight.

So may we here as we gather together in friendship
Sing praises to God and each one feel uplifted
Be led by the Spirit to do Thy work rejoicing
Over the hillside with lamps filled and lighted.

In our younger days in Sunday school
We would be taught to listen to His Word
At times we would concentrate and do our best
Then take it easy as we needed a rest.

But as we get older, these times flood back in our mind
We feel very grateful to our teachers who were so kind.
We perhaps did not want it, because we wanted to play
Now years have passed on, but then we had no say.

So let us continue to serve our Lord Jesus with goodwill
And keep our lives progressing and faithfully do His will
It is at times when feeling low we turn to God for advice
Because it was on the Cross our Saviour paid the sacrifice.

So as we remember the pain our Lord Jesus went through
To save the lost sinners, which that means, me and you.
May we rejoice by proclaiming our Saviour is living, not dead
And know Him from the start, not just at the breaking of bread.

Roy Truman

Magical Norway

Vast and overpoweringly beautiful,
Where the magnificent music of Grieg
Blends with the rushing sound of waterfalls
Cascading off the rugged mountain tops.
Charm and legend long prevail.

Still guarded by ghostly warrior hordes
Who from Valhalla roust all latent threats
She treasures every acreage of land,
But her inner soul is of the high seas,
Her arteries the fjords.

Though sombre are the haunts of evil trolls
Tucked away in darkest banking forest,
And barren are the lands of 'The Midnight Sun'
Where Thor still hammers distant dreams of Man,
Charm and legend long prevail.

Richard J Bradshaw

Bertie

Bertie was a beetle and he lived inside a church,
High up on the rafters was his customary perch.
He sometimes came to service in his shiny black-tailed coat
And scared the lady organist by landing on a note.

He was partial to a nice oak beam or even one of pine,
Though he wasn't too particular on what he chose to dine.
He frightened little spiders by saying to them - 'Boo!'
And in alarm they'd scuttle off not knowing what to do.

He'd wait until the choirboys were sitting in their places
Then, he'd walk upon their books and pull quite awful faces.
If they started laughing and the vicar wore a frown
He'd stand up on his front two legs and go on upside down.

But weddings were his favourites, the ones he liked the best,
He'd just pop up at random and try to scare each guest.
The nervous ones among them would let out a stifled shriek
While Bertie sat there chuckling at his own confounded cheek.

His behaviour at a christening was all that one could want,
Save the time he overbalanced and fell into the font.
He propelled himself upon his back and sang 'Row for the Shore'
Which the vicar, turning crimson, decided to ignore.

He really was a menace though he had a lot of fun,
The wardens never caught him because they couldn't run.
He would make a lovely ticking noise though no one knew where from
And once the church was emptied cos they thought there was a bomb.

One day a sharp-eyed cleaner saw him scuttle down the aisle
And she got him in the Hoover with a most un-Christian smile
'Beware your sins will find you out,' is something you can trust
Or you might end up like Bertie and have to bite the dust!

Kay Kisby

When I Leave

When I leave this world behind
Please do not be sad for long,
Dry your eyes, deep breath, blow your nose
You know it upsets me when you cry
Cry, but not for long.

Remember all the happy times
We helped each other
Building an everlasting tapestry
How happy you made me
The love I had I leave with you
An invisible circle lingering on.

In its strength you will grow strong
I know I've been there, it does not die
Renew your strength as days go by
Never forget how much I loved you
Do not be afraid, emotion is love
So maybe cry a little more.

Soon enough you will smile again
As you now hold the tapestry we built
I'm not so far away my dearest love
Soldier on, pass on this love
You are stronger than you think
Be at peace, relax, let your heart sing out again
Remember there's some of me in you
Your ever-loving mum.

Liz Dicken

Think Kindly

Soon the allotted time will come of death
Do not remind me
And if then maybe you think of me
Think kindly.

Harsh words have oft been spoken
But these are now all behind me
So if and when you think of me
Think kindly.

A bad one I am really not
Though some do malign me
Nevertheless, if you think of me
Please think kindly.

Others see me in a different light
But I am how He designed me
And if they think of me at all
Perhaps they'll think kindly.

Lucky me blessed with love
Having you close beside me
Hope that you will, thinking of me,
Think kindly.

Someone like you I'd long waited for
And hoped that you would find me
Remember me now and please, somehow,
Think of me kindly.

Les Dale

Reflections

Mirror mirror on the wall
silent witness to it all

Each in turn they take their place
before your bland immobile face

The youthful ones with eyes afire
all expectation and fierce desire

Some will live in fortune's favour
that licensed thief of others' labour

Some build castles in the air
then let the rooms to the unaware

Some will love and to their cost
should fate decree their paradise lost

But most will find they have to chance
the fractured road of circumstance

So mirror mirror it's just your task
to reflect no more than each passing mask

For if traced to you illusions shattered
soon as shards would you be scattered.

G F Hawkes

To A Dear Friend Who Died Of Alzheimer's

Dear friend, why have you left me?
Why did you have to go?
For years we shared our joys and sorrows
But now for us no more tomorrows.
For you have changed, God show me why
Explain the reason, heed my cry.
About me now I see such sadness
To share with you no hint of gladness
Your loved ones cry, you do not care
I talk to you, you stand and stare
Can this be right, a mind so changed
God help me please to understand.

I M Grutt

Country Colours

Cereal crops of soothing green,
Richest yellow oil seed rape,
Strokes as with an artist's brush
Laying plots of varied shape.

Canopied with blue and white
Puff-ball clouds in lofty skies,
Black the soil which frames the fields,
Distances that draw the eyes.

Birdsong carried on the breeze
Singing all the daylight hours,
Small white houses here and there
Bright front doors with garden flowers.

Golden sunshine over all
Feeds and nurtures Mother Earth
How I love thee peaceful Fens
Ever true - land of my birth.

Gwen C Wilbourne

Armageddon Was Yesterday

Rats by the million, cockroaches too,
Why's the sky orange? It used to be blue.
Why is my skin all purple and red?
Why are the bodies all tortured or dead?
It just couldn't happen, this nuclear war,
'We're safe with these weapons,' the leaders all swore.
But those still living wished they were dead
With nothing to live for, a place of sheer dread.
What of the unborn awaiting their fate?
For the mutations no future awaits.
No one to aid them, no one to save
Their misery stretching from cradle to grave.
The rich had their shelters, they were all right
The simple had nothing save only for flight.
But the poor had it better if only they knew
The rich just died slower midst buckets of spew.
So the cockroach was left alone on the Earth
Responsible now for the planet's rebirth.
The master of nothing but Man's desecration
To struggle and strive for a better creation.

Ray Walker

No Place Like Home

I've travelled the world - yes, I'm lucky I know,
All those wonderful sights, but wherever I go
The thought that prevails round the world as I roam
Like Dorothy says, 'There is no place like home.'

I've sailed in a junk on Honk Kong's China Sea
And Bangkok in Thailand's a great place to be.
The Seychelles are fabulous waters so blue
Those Caribbean islands are beautiful too.

I've been off to Canada - Niagara Falls
Hawaii too hearing those 'aloha' calls.
Los Angeles, California, San Francisco too
But old England is home to me I'm telling you!

I've sailed around Norway - my, that was some fun
Seen wonderful northern lights and midnight sun
We've sailed on the Danube and also the Rhine
Done the Greek islands - of course that was fine.

Madeira and Tenerife in a timeshare
Had wonderful holidays staying out there.
And there's times out in Portugal and also in Spain
Then we fly back one more to England - and rain!

I've travelled the world - yes, lucky me,
With its peoples and exotic places to see.
But give me old England wherever I roam
And as Dorothy said, 'There's no place like home.'

Kath Hurley

A Secret Place

I have a place not very far
where dreams and memories live
and often when I'm on my own
I got there and I sieve
through dreams at first as they're not real
 but full of joy and laugher
dreams of love and dreams of smiles
and peace for ever after.
A tranquil life where all is good
and no one ever breaks the rules
happiness is the main thing there
and everyone suffers fools.

Then I turn to memories
some are really sad
some are happy, most are good
but others really bad
they all relate to how we feel
in that we're not united
the fact is that they are all real
and we are all short-sighted.
Jealousy rears its ugly head
which is a mortal sin
poverty keeps appearing
and temper's wearing thin.
Selfishness is another fault
and pride is hovering near
following that there are three more traits,
hatred, greed and fear.
These ingredients for our life
are not too good it seems
so here I am all on my own
left only with my dreams.

J Ellis

The Metronome

Poor monstrous heart that still beats time
Way beyond the common years,
Poor mindless tyrant, master over
Failing limbs and eyes and ears.

As age undoes our bold attempts
To show we're more than pulp and bone,
Humiliation's more prolonged
By nature's cruel metronome.

Impatience and pity silently fight
As you eye the approaching shadowed night.
Time the night came, time to be gone,
And impatience and pity at rest in the urn.

Time now to hear those measured words
That bring some peace as you depart,
And hope - that not oblivion
But kindness, greet the worn-out heart.

Gillian Judd

Memories

I wish I could ask you questions, I never got to ask,
Or ask you to forgive me, for taking you to task.
I wish I could hold you and stroke your fevered brow,
Now that you are gone my dear, I cannot do that now.
There is an empty space within my heart; no one else can fill,
So much so - that every night, I dream about you still.
I hear your voice and see your face, as if you're still right here,
In the house, the things I do, the things I touch, seems to bring you near.
As I lay in my lonely bed, I bid you a fond goodnight,
And wish my arms could hold you in warmth till morning light.
But, I cannot do that now, I only wish I could and take once more
Our Sunday walks along the prom, close by the sandy shore.
And walk back home, call into shop or buy an ice from the van
By the esplanade slope, oh what a pleasure that would be, I can
See it now, like it was yesterday, a treat in the summertime
After the walk along the prom and up the slope's steep climb
Chatting as we strolled along, about the boats we saw, way out at sea
Or, the kids, building sandcastles and parents taking tea.

Kenneth V Jackson

Glance My Way

It doesn't pay to look over at someone on the way home from work. *(Pause)*
It is not worthwhile.

Those fifteen minutes of travelling together we make our games of make-believe.
A glance is not worthwhile.

Your tongue is made redundant, no speech required.
You look as well, and wonder what is it all about.

We both think I am doing wrong but it's something we will never find out.

I am too afraid to talk because it will all come out wrong.
The guy who sits with you, whom I like, and I am sure he has gotten me wrong.

Is it him I want to talk to?
Can you help? Can you make him see me?

Did you pity me with that gaze the other day when I was trying not to look
Or did you want to speak with me but you dare not really look?

I saw you walk to work today; you *stopped, looked and stared*
You glanced. Where will this lead and where will it end?

But your friend, (I call him Ted) he is the one I missed?
You know I missed his smile, his glance, a look.

I only thought about *you* but ignored poor Ted who just sat next to you reading
his book.
Is he my future? I will give him *a glance, a stare and maybe a look.*

Darren Morley

Nosey Sun

The sun glares through the old woman's window
Reminding her that she is still alive not merely a widow.
'OK, OK, I see you,' she moans sitting up in her bed.
'Go away Sun before I see red.
How dare you intrude in my misery!
Why you are so bright is a mystery.
I know you want people to be happy probably
But you can count me out surely.
Don't you remember '1996' when my soulmate was killed by Zeus?
Fourteen years of emptiness
Thanks to this God's clumsiness.
We were happy and didn't do anyone any harm
He was my reason for living so full of charm.
Anyway, I sat up didn't I Sun?
Now go away and elsewhere have fun.
Go after Zeus and have a row with him if you like
Go on, shoo, shoo, on your bike.'

Thus said the old woman laying back again in her safe nest
Clutching the picture of her lost sweetheart (Ronnie) to her chest.
Pulling a face, the sun vanished behind a cloud
He could have persisted but it was a waste of time he said aloud.
Instead he went to see this Zeus she mentioned earlier on
And asked him why he tore those people apart and for what reason.

Sylvette Gilbert-Sivieude

Faces

The things you seem to say
To me
Mean not much to you
But me
A thousand words are spoken
Just in the way
You look at me
Done wrong
Have I
Speak true
For I
Must know
The truth.

Thomas Baker

Migraineur

It comes like a thief in the night
To rob me of my sanity,
As I lay, just beneath consciousness,
It prowls, hiding in the dark shadows of my fear.
It stalks, watching, waiting, wanting to posses me,
To claim me as a victim of its power and unrelenting terror.

The mists of my troubled sleep evaporate
Revealing the monster within.
While a tidal wave of nausea engulfs me
And explosions blast agonisingly inside my skull,
It tears down my flimsy defences
Cracking my outer shell with an iron fist
As it penetrates the core of my existence.

Like a demon from Dante's Inferno
It torments me
Wildly screaming in my fragile ears
As my brain swells and pulsates
From this unforgiving entity.

Gathering strength, this malevolent force rages,
My resistance is shattered,
And I am at the mercy of my adversary
Its vice-like grip holding me prisoner.
Now, my body, weakened and limp,
Craves for release, even death.

But the world around me, inside me
Spins faster and faster into an all consuming madness, suffering
Endless pain
Pain
Intolerable pain.

Razor-sharp teeth rip through my skin, muscle and bone
Splaying open my vulnerability for its pleasure
Cruel fingers gouge out my eyes
And all I see are the fires of Hell
Its flames searing into my mind
Parading grotesque images of eternal torture.

Punishment is relentless
Like a sailor lashed to the mast of his ship
Flesh laid bare,
For the strike of the whip
Slicing, splitting
Blow after blow
Pain
Intolerable pain.

Writhing, convulsing, losing touch with my identity
My face disappears and is remoulded
Into a contorted grimace
As the beast takes up residence.

Three days and nights my mind and body wander in purgatory
As the beast strips away my humanity.
And always
Pain
Intolerable pain.

Then, at last,
Peace comes
Freedom from hurting,
My returning soul emerges into the soft subdued room
As the echoes of the vanished foe
Recedes and dissipates through the walls,
Satisfied with the penance paid,
It releases my spirit back to life and the living.

Carrie ann Hammond

Asia Incontinent

Amidst the statuary of mortar boards
Professing a credo of greed
And lava of stratified society
Totally unsupported by the construction
Of a unified heart
Which finds pinnacles of success
Only when sharing.

Polarised we stand as magnets
Distracted by all that we experience
Apart by the laws that dictate
That an ego should have autocracy
So walruses sing among the boughs of thoughts
And shapes turn into the fantasies of albatrosses
Upon leaden skies
The legacy of a world without substance
Except that it should matter.

D Jones

The Silent Night

So still the night
How cold the air
Where are you now?
I do fear

For your life
This world is full of so much strife
Oh little one
Sweet child your lips and large brown eyes
Gently you breathe your gentle sighs

You are but one year old
No sad stories to be told
No sad stories to behold
But they will come as sure as you
Will grow and grow true and true

Sweet child sleep tight,
This still dark night
I'll leave by you a lantern bright
To keep you warm this still dark cold night

Gentle dreams you will dream
As the night goes on it seems
This cold dark night
Make stars shine bright
Oh little one sleep tight.

Gloria Preston

Strange In Every Way

In the times we live all you see each day
Is iPods, TVs, computers, constantly changing our ways,
Some things we do, they're all we use
They are simply there for us to abuse.

I am seventeen, seen the gadgets change,
The years haven't been long, but what we have now is strange.
When I was small, you were lucky to own
A PC computer in your own home.

Laptops, Blue-ray, mp3
Things we use, never for free.
As the gadgets come out we need to stash
Our money for expense, use our cash.

They have been changed but it isn't the end
Machinery and gadgets are Man's best friend.
In twenty years we would look back to today
And think the current gadgets are strange in every way.

Teri Manning

Daddies

They're daddies little boys
They are not some toys
They will also learn
You have to earn
Don't stay at work
Cos you don't want to shirk
They will be taught
They have your support
Just stay in tune
They still have you
Don't be so sad
They will be glad
Cos you are their dad
These little lads
They're wonderful boys
With lots of toys
Cheer up my lad
You're a wonderful
Dad.

Rita Joel

Last Song

Black dye socialises with the sweat on the singer's face
as his unsteady voice grabs for the once easy heights.
Fingers that had caressed a hundred eager bodies now twist
like ivy around the mike, barely able to cling with conviction.
The audience shift and fidget through a tasteless love-song
and cringe as he shakes arthritic hips -
the last stab from his unpressed trousers proving too much.
When the final word from the final song staggers around the hall
it finds no playmates, and so hides and dies in solitude.

Gaye Giuntini

Judge Not

It is a lovely day
Buds are bursting
Sun is shining
Spring is on the way.

Life can be so good
Look ahead
Don't look behind
It's no use if you could.

Summer gives its gentle heat
We love the warmth
The longer days
Let us savour the treat.

Leaves fall gently to the ground
Bright colours glow
Days drawing in
Harvests gathered in around.

Winter comes with waning moon
Bare trees rest
Earth must wait
All creatures accept a slower tune.

The years gone all too soon
The seasons had their sway
Morning, evening, midnight noon
Marching time has its way.

So this is my philosophy
Live each day as it arrives
Learn from mistake and try
Never to judge other's lives.

Margaret Deverson

August

Tonight the star no longer shines
The stage is empty
Dancing shoes
And tutus
Unadopted.

Lights
Music
Applause
Silenced.

Our star appears elsewhere tonight
Added to the galaxy.
Such greed
And arrogance
To snatch our earthy light
And plunge within
That myriad star shine.

Fools
To think our star
Would not out-shine
Their meagre light
And more.

The star is not on stage tonight
Crowds linger
Pointing fingers
Whispers
Gossip
She didn't eat.

Success wed failure
In one night
No curtain call
No bouquets
By request
The star is gone
To shine elsewhere.

Robyn Dalby-Stockwell

Lest We Forget

Remember this day, remember it well,
In one brutal hour ten thousand men fell.
Ninety long years - a lifetime ago,
But they were our men and we loved them so.

Over clover and poppy machine gun took aim
Mortally wounding again and again,
Mingling with lime dust and sparkling dew
Fell the first drops of life blood, bright crimsoned hue.

The cannons roared and the bullets whined
And the screaming shrapnel pierced mankind,
Gasses of mustard and phosgene swirled by
Choking the lungs and blinding the eye.

Thunderous explosions dulled their despair
As cordite and lyddite tainted the air,
Wave after wave they braved the onslaught
Though endless the courage - their young lives how short.

Amidst stagnant water and trembling ground
Trench walls collapsed with barely a sound,
Incessant hot metal screamed through the sky
And the unseeing dead, stared with unseeing eye.

The injured - so many, entangled in wire
Broken bodies lay grotesque and still in the mire,
Soldier on soldier in mad disarray,
Surely the gates of Hell opened that day!

Week after week the battle raged on
A quarter of million brave warriors gone,
Remember this day with sorrow and pride
For there on the Somme so many men died.

Now white crosses gleam in the gentle sun
And hushed is the birdsong about each one,
Be proud of our brave lads and quiet your weeping
Then slowly pass by - our soldiers are sleeping.

J Burrows

Today, Yesterday

The modern world - the world today
Gismos to the right - gismos to the left
Much more crime and much more theft
Of values we seem to bereft
A society of self - of the big me
Family values in decline
Indoors no fresh air - online
No good trying to live in the past
Switch on, tune in, give it a blast
Progress, what is that you may say?
Better in the past or better today
Children in doors not out at play
Is it yesterday - today - or tomorrow
That is here to stay?

Clive Cornwall

Afterwards

It was the stillness that I loved
And the quietness of a passion spent.
Yet earlier the downpour had thrilled -
Pounding, beating on my windows -
Hissing, thrusting, urging me to listen.
And when I'd done so it could rest
And soften into the whispered breathing of a sleeping lover.

And afterwards
A chaffinch sang.

Anne Cotton

Kohima - A Last Goodbye

Before Kohima made a stand
young men who on a hillside sleep,
far, far from their native land
when loved ones for lost years weep.
There is a rugged cross of teak all
who come may stand in prayer
with hymn and sermon solace seek
or shed for them a silent tear.

As evening falls soft breezes sigh
o'er men with honour for their crest
a hushed and whispered last goodbye
may they eternal ever rest.
Where sweet scented flowers grow
on Norfolk Terrace side of hill,
from river valleys far below
drifting mists make time stand still.

Within the sound of battle cry
were there ever none so brave
as those that fought for you and I
for peace we've known and long may have
aggression they went out to fight
so we would be free to say
for all men to have this right
gave their tomorrow for our today.

W Fisher

Silent Screams

Baby Peter, pudding and pie,
Why did no one hear when they made you cry?
When the social workers came out to play
Why didn't they see your pain hidden away?

Their eyes were open, but closed too tight
To the torture you were put through every day and night
Society is guilty too for all the children just like you
Victoria Climbie went through the same thing too
Tortured to death, still nobody knew.

Silent screams behind closed doors
When the children come out today
Look and see, don't turn away
When you hear a child's cry, look even closer, find out why
Don't let your eyes be open but cannot see,
Help the children like Baby P.
Shock, horror, we read it all
So why does no one make that call?

Doctors who fail to see broken bones on Baby P
What kind of medical professional can you be?
You couldn't diagnose his agony
Don't be scared, help save a life
Do what you know is right
Tell the NSPCC of the poor child's plight.

Unlike Social Services they will not be deterred
They would rather remove a child to stop them being hurt.
Better than them ending up in a grave beneath the dirt
Remember all the children from A to Z
That's the legacy of Baby P.

Annette Foreman

Hundreds Of Rooks

Rise up together
effortlessly from their rookery in Reydon

From the high tops of the outstretched tree twigs
They take off
soaring into the air
where they wheel, and circle round,
clockwise and counter clockwise
expertly and with familiarity
using the air currents
like a vortex
evidently enjoying the *'whoosh'*
of their experience.

Gradually dispersing, in ones or twos flying out
in lines to differing predetermined directions
where various awaiting cornfields lie.

The harvest has been taken;
the fields are left rich for the picking
with fallen grain.

The collective identity of the 'parliament'
engenders every bird with knowingness,
understanding and wellbeing.

Both individual bird and rook as a part of the whole
continue to
survive, vital and alive,
as nature intended.

Victor Weston

Childlike Beauty, Childlike Trust

Soft supple skin, so downy to the touch
Large trusting eyes, not expecting much
Just tender love and care given throughout each day
From mothers, fathers, carers, in a tender loving way

Small dimpled hands on outstretched chubby arms
Raised in simple trust to be cuddled, loved and calmed
To be given the assurance throughout each passing day
That they are loved and needed throughout life's earthly way

Rosebud mouths and lips, dainty little ears
Learning how to talk from what each day they hear
What sort of words and languages will they hear from day to day?
What will those dainty mouths and lips learn to speak and say?

It may not be just little ones who need our care each day
But those a little older who need to share, but cannot say
Because each day is busy, we haven't got the time
To put our arms around them and tell them they'll be fine

No matter what our sex or age life has its ups and downs
We need that special person to be there, be around
To give advice and courage, give a helping hand
To make themselves available, to listen and understand

God has given life and breath, and placed into our care
Every single child, no matter who or where
It's our responsibility throughout life's earthly way
To show them love and tenderness today and every day.

Dorothy Durrant

Text Elope

Why r we 4 for
tea? wen all I
want is you 4
me. Keep it brief
now don't say
much, costs a
fortune such &
such. Speed is of
the essence
now, if u want 2
save a row. Luv
u 2; fly with me,
economy 2 isle
capri. xxx

Delia Marheineke

Outing To East Mersea, Essex Coast

Morning waves of cow parsley rolled apart
as we sliced through the flat lane.

Sand martins skimmed a strip of beach squealing.
A skylark outfaced the wind against a purple sky.
Giant oaks, in slow suicide, slipped
where skeleton-trunks lay beached, like whales.
Bubbles of sea-campion strained for lift-off in the low breeze.

Evening foam of cow parsley fizzed back,
a wake to mark our passing.

Hazel Dongworth

A Kind Of Love

He stalked into my life a pint-sized inquisitive
Dark-hard bundle, cocky ready to stake his place
Within our home, then, with an air of approval he
Claimed me, they said that I didn't like cats but
That was untrue. I respected their freedom of spirit
And independent nature. He required only one more
Asset to champion his cause, and chose myself for
Reasons unknown. He would meet me at the garden gate
On my homecomings. Climb me as he would a tree and
Whisper in my ear, *hello Dad.* His intelligence seemed
To have no bounds. A blow to one ear caused it to fold
The other a symbol a feather. As an Indian brave he was
Fearless with intruders, he checked everything that I did
Around the home. He spoke to me of his wants through my
Mind and thanked me. It was a kind of love that left me
Wanting to understand. For it was genuine and honest over
Eighteen years. Years of dreams to share within our
Home and garden and at our final parting his eyes told
Me all I needed to know that the line between cat and
Man can be broken. For we were as one in life and death.

Ronald Blaber

The Coastal Path
(Walking the Pembrokeshire coastal path)

Since early morn we had walked
My companion and I,
Sometimes together; sharing thoughts,
Other times apart: happy in solitude.

The rain had stayed with us
Like an unwelcome guest:
Dancing on hoods, dripping down necks,
Saying no to the rests that we longed for.

The path: once dry and bold -
Now played games with our boots
That fought hard in clinging mud,
Heavy-soled: a luckless task.

To land, the brambles tore and clung,
To sea, the cliffs dropped crazily
Always there, menace to progress,
Reminding what a slip would cost.

The heavy rain and mist
Obscured the postcard views,
The sights that first had lured us
To hike this coastal path.

Even the crash of waves on rocks
Two hundred feet below us,
Was often lost: both sight and sound
By battering wind and tearing rain.

Hours passed and no respite
From damp and cold and hunger,
We wondered where the pleasure lay
In such a holiday as this.

Then from our clifftop path
We saw through broken clouds,
A golden thread some miles away:
Newgale Beach, between land and sea.

With something now to aim for
We quickened up our pace,
Both knowing without need to tell
The place where we would stop.

Arriving at the long white beach,
Pushed hard by Atlantic waves
And held firm by Silurian rocks,
We slowed our pace at last.

The smooth, clean, virgin sand
Stretched dazzling before us,
Where horses' hooves alone had trod,
No sign was there of human.

In wind and rain and now sea spray
We crunched the untrod sand,
And felt, despite the sweat and toil,
This alone made all worthwhile.

Nigel Whitesides

If Winter Comes

If winter comes will you be there beside me?
Will you be there, when frost nips all my dreams?
When cold winds blow and snow falls all around me
And the sun no longer sends its warming beams.

I need to feel your hand in mine to comfort,
To see you smile, when everything is grey.
To hear you speak with calming reassurance,
To give me strength to face another day.

When the springtime of my life is far behind me,
When summer's gone and autumn nears its close,
Will you be there close by my side to guard me
And bring to me that last sweet fragrant rose?

Amelia Wilson

Seasons

Winter world is snowy white
Jack Frost weaves his spell at night,
Glowing fires their shadows cast,
Christmas time is here at last,
As winter slowly fades away,
Spring shows her face again in May.

Spring is here so give a shout,
All the flowers have blossomed out.
Colours of the rainbow blend,
To nature's magic there is no end.
April showers come and go,
People hurry to and fro.
Windows open to the air, flowers scented everywhere.

Summer sunshine warms the land,
Let us join the happy band.
Faces tilted to the sun,
Happy faces everyone.
Mother Nature at her best,
Stop a moment, take a rest,
A host of memories to store yours to keep for evermore.

Softly, softly autumn creeps
Nature's secret sure to keep.
Toning colours of a golden hue
Autumn garb is nothing new.
Softly blending gold to brown,
Summer leaves come tumbling down.
Soon the trees stand straight and bare
Waiting for the crisp night air.
Fires once again glow bright, ready of the winter night.

Valerie M Helliar

Devon's Shore To Shore

It has a North it has a South
But not an East and West
The shoreline of our country
Is beautifully dressed

The patchwork quilt of greens and browns
Atop the moors and dales
Set off the coastal ruggedness
With distant views of Wales

Our shores have many facets
In winter cool and grey
When wind and waves are dancing
Competing in their play

Devon's coast is beautiful
Its history abounds
The Pilgrim Fathers left from her,
Sailing out of Plymouth sound

A lovely walk along the shore
Is from the Valley of the Rocks
To Lynton and to Lynmouth
Where disaster once did knock

The rivers rush to exit
From the coastline all around
The Dart, the Taw and Torride
Are but a few that can be found

Our favourite beach is Instow
With Appledore beyond behind
The boats moor on the sand it seems
But no one seems to mind

So there you have our shorelines
With their gifts we've never poor
From cliffs to sunny beaches
Variety galore.

Carole Hurst

A Dark, New Day

A dark cloud hangs over my head,
I pull my aching body from my bed,
I wonder, if the phone will ring,
I wonder, what news it will bring,
I wonder, what the postman will bring,
And will this winter ever turn to spring,
Oh how I like to hear the songs of the birds that sing.
The fun and laughter of the children has gone,
The only enjoyment is the birds' sweet song,
And when it's cold, even that is gone.
I wake each day full of despair,
I run a comb through my old grey hair,
I turn on the TV, and what do I see,
Death and destruction for all to see,
The newspaper drops through the front door,
I open the pages, and I wonder,
What for, death, destruction is all that I saw,
A mugging, a stabbing, killings galore,
I close the paper, just cannot read any more,
I force myself to open the front door,
I close it quickly, I cannot take any more,
It seems my life, has become a great chore,
The phone starts to ring, it makes my heart jump,
Who could be ringing this old grey lump,
A sweet voice on the phone,
Lets me know I'm not alone,
I open the curtains, a light shines through,
I suddenly realise, I have much to do,
I feel much better, I know I will get through,
It's just the start of a day that is new.

M K P Smith

War Baby

A bolt of dove-grey silk
ruffles the early morning sky
then slides away.

The ice skate tracks of aircraft trails
criss-cross each other,
soften and diffuse
to lambswool curls.

A sheep rolls on its back
like a cob set free of its harness,
then rights itself and falls on its knees
to graze the downland scrub.

My heartbeat tread
kicks out sequestered Sunday lines:
'And all the blue ethereal sky'.
Just one small cloud,
stretched to a sea-snake's wily shape,
swims on to drink its fill
and spill a shock of summer rain.

Around my head a fat bee's Spitfire whine,
while in among the dusty weeds of summer
bright-eyed poppies bay for blood.

Ann Segrave

Memories

When I was small I do recall a satin dress of pink.
It was a wedding that I wore this lovely dress I think.
I also had a hat of straw with roses round the brim.
It had a ribbon on the side to tie beneath my chin.

My shoes were black and ankle strap, patent now I guess.
Of all the people that were there, I thought I looked the best.
Going to my nana's was a very special treat.
Plonking on the pianoforte, sitting on the seat.

It was made of horsehair colourful in hue.
Everything she had was old, nothing there was new.
She did not have a wireless, or a telephone,
Yet beside the piano was a wind up gramophone.

'The Laughing Policeman' was a record that we played a lot.
I really liked it best of all, I never have forgot.
He laughed and laughed, until we all were really laughing too.
Yes! I loved my nana and the things we used to do.

Something else that comes to mind that now we never see.
She had a big old mangle in the scullery,
With wooden rollers and a handle, that was as big as me.
It took a lot of effort to turn it round and round,

But if my brother helped me it made a grating sound.
The rollers creaked and groaned a lot with washing squeezing through.
It really pushed the water out; but made me all wet too.
Yes! I loved my nana and the things she let us do.

When I started school I took a penny for a bun.
It was the year when bottled milk was free for everyone.
When we went to war of course; different then we know.
Sitting in the shelter when the sirens used to go.

A smell of bricks and mortar; dark and damp and so;
Lessons missed, songs were sung, for nowhere else to go.
The whine of doodlebug and bomb; I do remember well.
That is past and nowadays one does not like to dwell.

Food was short in time of war that I do recall.
We kept chickens in our yard behind the garden wall.
The cockerel was a bully and wasn't nice at all.
Whenever we collected eggs he always chased me out.
I never ever, volunteered if others were about.

My mother used to hatch the eggs inside out oven range.
Little balls of golden fluff, I thought it rather strange,
That sometimes she just cooked the eggs and ate them for our tea.
If it was a special day, a chicken it would be

We also liked the cinema, much better than today.
Besides the films and newsreel, an organist would play.
The lights would dim; the organ then; would rise up from below.
Like some glass throne, its changing colours, gave a magic glow

My memories hold special thoughts; I hope they never fade.
I grew up in wartime when history was made.
Momentous times and happy times, I remember well.
I wonder what the future holds! Only time will tell.

Molly Phasey

Untitled

To Donna,

The day I came to you I had reached an all time low,
But seeds of your treatment certainly began to sow,
To completely relax was so very hard to do,
But you were so kind and compassionate and you were just being you.
I felt for the first time that maybe I could give
More of my inner self, so that I could live
A different life than I had been for so many years
Even though during the treatment I never gave way to tears
I held something back, in control I have to be
I wish I could be different, maybe one day I'll see
That the way you help people is to live life a different way
To be happy in the present and live life from day to day.

Love Sue.

Sue Holcroft

Bromley Berries

I am a gardener of great renown
and travel the shows from town to town,
thirsty for medals and cups and shields
but no regard for onions or peas
or anything below the knees like
cabbages, potatoes, leeks and swedes.
My bent is berries, I do not jest,
quite superior to all of the rest.

They say local gooseberries have always been
possibly, by far, the best you've seen,
and as for taste, there is little doubt
it's pick-of-the-bunch when I'm about!
Succulent, supreme, an artful dream,
sweetness sublime, you have to admit,
delicately flavoured, know what I mean
and such a glorious Sherwood green.

I take care, and have a useful knack
to render my currants huge and black.
The secret is to drape the bush
with nets against the pigeon, jay and thrush,
never to play at shotgun tactics
or similar serious antics,
but when I claim the God-given crop
I leave the birds some fruit on the top.

I'm clever with elderberry wine,
you won't find many as good as mine,
so richly ruby, well fortified,
I cheat a bit after fermentation,
do a second fortification,
two tablespoons of old French brandy
goes lightly into every flagon,

Did I hear right, you're on the wagon?

Alan Smith

The Sixties Cult

A glow in past history
A reality, no longer a mystery
The aftermath of war.
No more fields of mud
Regiment wiped out as they stood.
What was it for
This relentless war
Not a way to live anymore
From out of this the antithesis no less
A complete change of dress
Silken shirts, the Charlton, to adore
Short cropped hair
Couples entwined on stair
The Twenties, new tunes to be sung
The fleetingness of youth,
And life goes on
New dictators arise
No longer a surprise
We carry on and suddenly
Another war has begun
The inevitability of the Sixties cult
We will get there again
And peace will begin.

Joan Hands

I Look To The Cross

Yes I look to the Cross and what do I see?
It's a Cross that is empty for my Saviour is free
Yes He's free from all pain, all suffering too
That for me on the Cross my Saviour went through
With a crown of thorns around His head
His body was broken and there He bled
Yes I look to the Cross and what do I see?
It's the love that my Saviour had for me
Where He forgave my sins, where He saved me too
Where eternal life He gave me it's true
Yes I look to the Cross and what do I see?
It's the price that my Saviour paid for me
Yes not only then but still now it's true
My Saviour still loves me and I love Him too
Yes I look to the Cross and what do I see?
It's a Cross that is empty for my Saviour is free
Yes He's risen, He's alive and will always love me
Yes He's not on the Cross, my Saviour is free
For my Saviour is Jesus, God's only Son
Who when on the Cross a victory He won
Yes I look to the Cross and what do I see?
It's a Cross that is empty for my Saviour is free
Yes my Saviour is Jesus, He lives now it's true
Hallelujah what a Saviour my Jesus is too.

Royston Davies

Cherish The Love You Have

We should cherish the time we have together
For little do we know when it will cease
When trouble and calamity break out
We should enter the Lord's peace

Do not take each other for granted
But with praise and gratitude
To love, honour and adore
That should be the attitude

Be always there for one another
Whatever comes your way
Greet each other with a kiss and a smile
At the start of each new day

Learn to bear with one another
Even with the things that irritate
For when you can love each other that way
That's the start of something great

Look out for one another
Bring little pleasures of joy
Be it through a flower, a card
Or even a cuddly toy

When you learn the secret of loving
From the bottom of your heart
Help to nurture and let it flourish
And from it never depart

Make your mark upon this world
So when you go to God in glory
Others who remember you
For you, will always have a story.

Jean Hazell

Surprise Of Spring

Slowly out of the grass I see,
new flowers showing their little heads,
delicate primroses smiling beautifully,
soon to see a splash of colour on this flower bed.

Crocuses, a head of fairy tale bells,
caressing their way to hazy sunlight,
inhale deeply, savour the smell,
darkness near, nodding petals, sleep in the night.

A lamb gently nuzzles its ma,
cotton wool texture of its fur,
clings near to her, and won't stray far,
for he really loves her.

A sprinkling of blossom, apple white,
for new life to grow,
it seems so rapid, whilst out of sight,
nature in reality, we know.

Birds bring a new friend,
collecting twigs, a broken nest they mend,
a flurry of passion and love,
fly courting and cooing, high above.

Clouds drift hazily across the sky,
blowing gentle in the air,
an intake of breath, to give a sigh,
hardly disturbing the life on earth, we know to share.

A tabby cat, kisses its kitten,
raspness of the tongue it cleans,
its eyes slowly open, then truly smitten,
a bundle of soft fur, woken from a dream.

Colours so dainty as petals they unfold,
peering their way around to look,
warming in the sun, no longer cold,
their life history, written in a book.

For this we can be sure, you see,
Mother Nature never changed,
life forms, in all ways, beautifully,
everything exact and unarranged.

I could not imagine anything bad,
at this time, love shows true,
new beginnings, and not to be sad,
how at beauty, like this, could you be blue?

Fiona Smith

Falling In Love

As the storm grew nearer, I struggled
To cope with the closeness around me.
I couldn't escape the helplessness
That was like some strange toxicity.

I was falling into a chasm
So deep, beautiful and enticing.
I couldn't reach out and grasp the trees
Their blossom like sweet sickly icing.

Would the ground break me when I landed?
Would it wrap me in soft cotton sheets?
Would I see all my life before me
Or still hear my heart's fast pounding beats?

I somehow think that you will catch me,
With strong arms that will hug my tired soul.
Can life be any better than this
And have I reached my final true goal?

Barbara Pearce

Untitled

A soldier in Afghanistan
To his loved one he did write
Sincerest greetings to you I send
Though far across the sea
My love for you will never end
And in my thoughts, you'll always be
Then through the silence of the night
Across the desert sand
My heart rejoice I hear your voice
And gently hold your hand.

G W Goodban

Untitled

All you see is the painted smile
but look at the eyes for the inner truth.
We are our own creations from experience of life
manifestations of childhood and youth.
Look more closely at people you meet
see past the smile and understand some are oppressed.
A smile can present an unknowing mask
not all is evident don't be impressed
for behind the smile is everyone's pain
drawn deep from within but not plain to see.
We all think we know people and have the right to judge
I should know because I always thought I knew me.

Kevin Brett

Life In The Fast Lane

The pace of today seems to grow faster and faster
With little time to stop and chat with a neighbour
Enjoy relaxing in the garden
Going to a concert to listen to a choir or band
Spend time playing with the children in a park
Having a holiday at home or abroad
Watching a good film at the cinema
Reading an absorbing book
Going to a local museum or art gallery
Playing sport in the park or leisure centre
Spending time with God's family at church
Reading the Bible and praying to the Father
And finding out how to be a better person
Instead of wanting more money and power
We should work to make this world a peaceful place
With equal opportunities for everyone
To develop their talents and skills
With a secure and loving home to live in.

David Cooke

Ode To A Pet Dog

Your doggy gave so many years of love and devotion,
but now has gone to sleep.
I believe there are doggy parks in Heaven,
so your doggy would not want you to weep.
Such fun, such energy, such zest for life,
your doggy had for sure.
A good friend, giving unconditional love,
and will be remembered for evermore.
It is so sad to lose a four-legged pal,
but your doggy knew to the very end
How much it was loved and treasured,
and that you were his life-long friend.

Yvonne Chapman

Come Let's Celebrate

Come let's celebrate, Forward Press has the key of the door,
Never been twenty-one before. Over the years
She opened it for word-spinners of today seeking
The fame of those long ago. Peterboro' deserve a party,
Since Forward led new writers impelled to write by extending
A broad invite, hoping readers to excite as like fish on juicy words they bite.
Meditation, a revelation to sympathetic publishers imparted, who
In the literary field got them started. Quelling a poet's tears when
To their efforts their critique did steer, given a theme

Whilst to thirty lines they were confined, scribes sought good vibes,
To please the reading tribes. Editors up to their ears in compositions
Took no sides but reviewed scripts from all positions, working neutrally
With no inhibitions, yet true to old and new traditions.
Aware to each piece there was a theme set with a thirty line limit and
Occasionally more are allowed just hope the editors remain unbowed.
For writer and reader, it is a challenge they can't ignore,
Promoting furthering of good book lore and so often both

Heavily score. To those who have generously opened doors,
Let's offer congratulations for spreading the word among all
Literate nations, come on let down your hair, out of the window
Fling all care yes, let's do it for we have the time and do incline
Our joy to share, as well as magnums for a publisher cum laude,
Of the best French champagne, the kind of which
Not even connoisseurs can complain, so
Neither our stomachs nor heads may feel any pain.

Graham Watkins

Emotional Stress Fears

When I am on edge and worried,
I feel my emotions are hurried.
It makes me shake like a leaf,
And my hands and wrists go a bit weak.
    I will eventually make myself ill,
And won't be able to pay the bill,
I haven't done my will,
I used to have a penpal called Jill.
    I have a lot of panic attacks and cry at a drop of a hat,
It's like I want to hit out like a bat.
I wish more people would understand how I feel,
So I don't pull in an empty reel.
    I can't seem to concentrate on anything I do,
And this is all very true.
I just feel I cannot go on,
In my head I feel a beat of a drum.

Susie Bell

Photographs

A photograph is a picture you can always keep
You can look at it in the daytime
Or dream of it in your sleep
It can be of a favourite person
Or fun you've had at home
It can be of a beautiful city
Be it in London or in Rome
Then when you are feeling lonely
And you want to have some laughs
And in your home there's no one
Just look at your photographs.

Ena Andrews

The Four Seasons

Wayside birdsong becomes a chorus
Heralding the spring,
Multithroats at dawn awaken
And in harmony sing.
Joy is everywhere around
Signs of nurtured growth abound.

Leaping lambs skip o'er the meadow
Dressed in verdant green,
Buds burst forth from dormant winter
Aching to be seen.
Joy is everywhere around
Signs of nurtured growth abound.

Lengthened days with summer weather
Heated by the sun,
Morning haze and midday breezes
Life forever fun,
Pleasure hours for all to find
Each their own selected kind.

Evenings made for melodious music
Sweetened with good wine,
Barbecues and strawberry teas
Time enough to dine.
Pleasure hours for all to find
Each their own selected kind.

Autumn leaves fall gently earthwards
Wisps of rusty brown,
Tree-lined avenues edge beauty
Nature's radiant gown.
Loveliness beyond compare
Manifest for all to share.

Shadows lessen as days shorten
Sunset's golden glow,
Woodland walks are scenic splendour
Autumn dictates so.
Loveliness beyond compare
Manifest for all to share.

Winter's chill clasps all around it
Often with ice and snow,
Birds and wildlife flee before it
Instinctively they know.
Time for fires and warmer wear
Frosty morns and trees all bare.

Footsteps crunch and foliage glistens
Tinselled by the sun,
Yet the crocus dares to peep
'Ere the winter's done.
Time for fires and warmer wear
Frosty morns and trees all bare.

Seasons come and seasons fade
Like the morning dew,
Pray enjoy them while you may
Before they bid adieu.
Each has beauty of its own
Temporarily to loan.

John Pert

Mortality

Unexpected, unaccepted, out of time
A mother's death at forty-two
What can I do?
Unexpected, unaccepted, out of time
A son at eleven weeks, he died too
A son at thirty, he died as he flew,
What can I do?
Unexpected, unaccepted, out of time.

Gael Nash

Impulsion

Who is to
Say what is
Good and what is
Bad -
If we are unmoved,
And feel we
Could do better -
That alone
Is enough to
Make that writer's
Work
Worthwhile.

Denise Harrison

Understanding

Sitting here thinking of times gone by
It was not easy I will not lie
A past with trouble and with strife
Not much different from my life
The years I know have flown by
Forgetting things I really try
When times get hard it makes me sad
Although my life is not so bad
I'm struggling in a different way
With what I cannot always say
A lack of understanding that is why
My illness though I cannot lie
Is here to stay I don't know why
But with some help I'm coping now
My illness though is here to stay
But I take my life day by day.

Manic depression.

Marion Dines

Edna

Out on her bicycle, into the four winds,
come rain or shine, Edna wends her way,
out of warm living room, into the face of morning,
up to the local shops, or off to do her cleaning.

Funny clinking sound, coming from the back rim,
oblivious to Edna, zipping down steep inclines,
breaks are not needed, head up gently gliding,
her skirt billowing will no doubt slow her down.

Edna picks up speed, she leans around the corners,
no effort needed, let the hill make the wheel spin,
a child again when her knees sniffed a summer's breeze,
her billowing skirt, cooling down the bicycle's engine.

Searching for the pedals, the wind sent them spinning,
bicycle swerving all over the road,
bag on the handlebar, swinging like a pendulum,
zipping on the wheel spokes, on leaning a bend.

Diced potatoes, the corner taken from the cheese,
front wheel spokes slightly bent but who gives a damn,
homeward journey, a little bit different,
having to walk up the hills, she easily came down.

She was like a river, she was ever flowing,
she was the stepping stones, we once crossed over,
with power and wit that made her so endearing,
Edna was more than any ordinary woman.

Somewhere in my mind in another dimension,
Edna works the pedals on a sunlit promenade,
down on the sandy beach, brother Bill is waving,
standing beside two deckchairs waiting to be filled.

Maurice Dennis Chater

Isle Of The Dead

Doré! Doré! Doré! Doest thou hear me,
My voice a-cracking the rheumy glass wide
Doré! Doré! Doré! Can you see, hear, be near
As I advance toward an incoming tide

Do you think for a moment, do you parade
This island retreat - what signifies, who the slave?
And should I hold a masked ball, where the cave?
Am I injured by some dubious lover's enslaved

Written large, spider-like, upon my back
How he grasped me, how he twisted me!
And kissing passionately, said, 'There is no looking back - all is black!'
Now I clear cobwebs, but no one pays my liberty's fee . . .

Doré! Doré! Doré! Dost thou hearest me?
For I shout through the gated bars of time
Doré! Doré! Doré! Why do you not let me free?
Who with a snap of fingers, could make gilded coins chime!

Yes! These whispery souls on the ebb of tide
Might try cave, rock pool, willow
In which to transport themselves - sense where to hide
What of Colette-kin-rider whose calm sleep lies shallow.

Upon the velvet cushion in coffined canopied box
Amidst the lost and the cursed
We keep abreast, on the least too much intoxicate
On the Isle of Thanet where gulls glide on unversed.

Joy Sheridan

Freedom

The parrot clings to the bars
of the castle's aviary. With
large white wings she soars.
High over the visitors' heads
into the blue sky above.
With mouths wide open,
they stare. As she makes
her bid for freedom.

J A Herbert

Congratulations Forward Press

F or twenty-one years, is it a time to remember?
O ver the decades the poets have passed by.
R elishing the style and tone of ancient men
W ords that flew first from an old quill pen.
A ncient lines, written with an olde poet's rhyme
R omancing the sounds that came from out of time
D rawing word pictures through the mind

P roviding chances for new poems to see the light
R emembering just how things began
E xciting word poems all clean and bright.
S howcasing a brand new life,
S o congratulations, to starting a new age.

Shirley-Patricia Cowan

Twenty-One Years

Forward Press is just the best
To send my poems to
To celebrate is so great
I feel that I am more a mate
I send my poems now and then
When I feel I can pick up my pen
When a thought comes into my head
I even write them whilst in bed
I'm doing this one, just for you.
To celebrate with love and laughter
And happy days forever after.
Congratulations, for a special year, your 21st
I'm so excited, I feel I'm going to burst!

June Gibson

Untitled

To celebrate a 21st
Makes you feel just great,
At last you've reached the dizzy height
That seemed so long a wait.

But now you're there and so grown up
You cannot think it's true,
The years it took to reach this day
Is this *really* you?

From birth to now has been such fun
With family and friends,
The in-between year memories
Have brought such different trends.

So have a drink on your great day
With food and fun galore,
Let's hope that as you celebrate
They'll be many, many more

Congratulations!

Joyce Hammond

Happy Feet

There's music playing down our street,
There's children running,
Hear their happy feet.

It's the ice cream van as you can guess,
A child starts calling,
I'm the next.

Some get lollies,
Some ice cream cones,
Some get sweets,
Others moan.

The children go and eat their treats,
There's no more running happy feet,
At least until tomorrow.

Glennis Ecclestone

Our Village

I love to hear the church bells ring
And to hear the choirboys sing.

Father John welcomes all his flock
Sunday morn at ten o'clock.

Down the road, across the green
Morris dancers can be seen.

The bells are ringing on their feet,
To stand and listen is a treat.

Village pub with seats outside
They sit and drink their beer with pride.

Old Farmer Tom will soon be here
He loves his pint of local beer.

So if you pass this way by bus
Stop off and have a glass with us.

Maurice Oliver

The Gulf Between

Once skilled proud hands.
Now, under used.
Grasp a can
on the arm of wearing sofa,
watching TV.

Thin, artistic hands.
Beyond frustration
grasp the pen,
that shaking, writes the note.
Hands that have never known
work above the minimum wage.

Gnarled, dirty hands,
stiff with cold.
Straighten the cardboard
beneath concrete.
Hands that once hovered over a trigger,
proudly serving Queen and country.

Finely manicured hands.
Slightly sweating,
grasp the wheel.
Tapping to latest sounds
trapped in traffic.
These hands transact millions,
knowing only RSI.

A practised hand
appears on TV.
Waving.
Fronting the smile
on the steps of Number 10.

The hand that grips the can
spills some down the grimy shirt.
Tears well in lost eyes
as his wife closes the door
leaving for work.

The hands that grips the pen
does not see,
does not care.
Finishes without a full stop.
Eyes only with a hollow stare
turn to take a final look,

The dirty hands
placed in groin (as trained).
Does not care.
Does not see
as he tries to sleep
behind the shop that sells TVs.

The manicured hands
safe within executive walls,
'Just a few friends round . . . that's all!'
Lifts the glass to the screen
saluting his champion.
For all to see . . .
   . . . and little changes in reality.

Kevan Taplin

Life

Life is a journey, as time goes by.
Hurrying by, like clouds, in the sky.
In hours, in days, in months, in years.
Some can be happy, others bring tears.
Fight the good fight,
When days are not right
Find time for each other
Sister or brother.
Every day is a bonus
As life hurries on
Even the days when
Something goes wrong.

K A Hollis

Bridie's Tale

Life's full of surprises, so they say
Out at 3.30am one day
Into a car with all the gear
Off to a champion show I hear

On we travelled in the dark
Maybe if I'm lucky we'll find a park
I curled up and went fast asleep
Now and again I took a peep

'You've gone the wrong way,'
I heard her say
Her friend said with a smile,
'We'll get back in a mile.'

Back on the right road once again
After leaving a country lane
I see a lot of lights up ahead
Surely it's not why I left my bed

On we went for miles and miles
'We're on the M25,' she said with a smile
I took a look out of the windowpane
And thought, hope they get in the right lane

Cars and juggernauts thundering by
As the dawn breaks, through the sky
That way, I heard her say to the NEC
Much rather had a cup of tea.

It's 7am and we arrive at the show
Off for a walk we went, and what do you know
Under a long tunnel we went
But could not find the hall, for the event

At last we found it, and our place
I looked at her with a smile on my face
A fur blanket was put on the bench you see
Then we all had that lovely cup of tea

Next to me was another red and white
And what a delight
He curled up his lips and smiled to me
It was love at first sight you see

We had both won prizes at the show
Then just as he flirted with me, wow!
My mistress said, 'Come on, time to go home.'
I went to sleep, all the way
Hoping to see him another day.

Joan Read

Home

A new house, a new home,
Time to settle, no more to roam,
Some new paint here,
Some new paint there,
A bit of filler on the stair.

It's so good, I want to shout,
This is what my life's about,
I've never settled down before,
Or even had my own front door,
To walk about from room to room,
There's peace and comfort, as in the womb.

The garden is a magical place,
Where birds and bees have their own space,
The lawn is very lush and green,
But to cut it, I am not that keen,
I just love the quiet around,
And the new contentment I have found.

This is home.

Kaye Coomber

In A Twinkling Of An Eye!

Birthdays come; birthdays go . . .
some come quick . . . some go slow;
yet in a twinkling of an eye,
your twenty years and one flew by!
Poets' thoughts, in words expressed
leaves the readers quite impressed
and freely use imagination;
to imbue a mystic fascination!
   Poems though - I often find,
seem to hide; but stay in mind,
then something somehow sets them free
to make a perfect symmetry!
   Rhyming rhythm can bring tears,
then soothing pictures ease appears,
while magic words of love implies
true devotion never dies!
   To read one's printed words completed
knowing nought has been deleted,
gives a sense of personal pride,
in which a love of verse abide!
   So go Forward . . . F Press - on in exultation
feel the joys of adoration;
and when all's been done and said . . .
review new poems and put to bed
to make a new and bright display,
to dedicate your special day!

P E Woodley

Cat And Sparrow

Suddenly
The cat went long
Thin
And froze in a pose that said silently
Do Not Touch
And then
Like a professional arrow out of a bow
The cat streaked across the openness of a well-kept lawn
For what
For the innocence of a small brown sparrow
A sparrow hurting neither man nor beast
But it flew off quickly
So quickly
And kept
In its flight
Its sparrow innocence

The cat shrunk back after that
Back to its previous fat
And became again
The inviting stroke-me-cat
While the sparrow perched on a high twig
Nodding to the great sparrow god
Its gratitude.

John Jones

Coming Of Age (1944/2009)

On *my* 21st birthday
I was stationed at Portishead.
My unit was defending Avonmouth Docks,
From the peril of bombers overhead!

The unit was on 'red' alert.
But I was given a special pass.
I rode the bus to Weston-super-Mare -
A grown-up woman at last!

The beach was mined and out of bounds.
The funfair silent and still.
So, a walk on the Prom, an hour in the pub
Along with a few strangers with an hour to kill.

As a 21st birthday, it *was* memorable,
But, all because it was wrong.
I made sure things were very different
When my children came along!

I'm certain *your* 21st birthday,
Will be full of congratulations and delight.
So, from one of your grateful contributors -
I'm cheering with all my might!

J M Jones

A Touch Of The Lips

With a touch of the lips it was love, it truly was, it was not
Just lust, it was so sweet and smelt of musk, my lady love
And I walked on air across the fields into the woods,
We climbed the hills to see the view, looking down at
The land to see where it ended, we imagined that we
Were in another world, away up in the sky, a place where
We could be alone in a friendly universe, high up among
The stars, where the mountains kiss the heavens and the
Moonbeams kiss the sea, so let there be just you and me
With our laughter flying through the trees like doves and
Let the world know that we are one not two and that as our
Lips touched we were bound together for all eternity.

Guthrie Morrison

Upon Her Chair

The old lady sat upon her chair
The years had gone where she knew not
Around the room possessions of a long lifetime
Precious to her, useless to others
Pupil of the school of life
She'd reached her highest grade
The wrinkled face showed experiences learned
Decisions made
No price for such things
Arthritis, weakness, depression, pain
A still young mind trapped in an aged useless body
Today's world no time to stand and stare
Rushing, rushing everywhere
Sentiment gone for good
What did they know with their sex and plastic money
She waited
No sound but the clock
Ticking those precious minuets
Heartbeats away from eternity
He would come for her as he did for everyone
What right to claim, hadn't he enough souls
The ghostly smile, his greed for death
The stranger all in black waiting at the door
At last they pass, the unsure hours of the night
The worst is over, the world still turns
The dawning and the light
The Grim Reaper will come someday but wait now he must
For life returns again, all is well
The old lady gave a smile, life is good.

Edward Warner

The New Work
(Of Wells and the Mendips)

The ash and the elm and the chestnut there,
Hold such cool, refreshing, moistening air
Now, while they stand there together, blending,
As no brush could ever share by lending,
To portray these peaceful scenes at morning,
When the night has gone and day is dawning.
The tractor splutters and its grinding blades
Turn forcefully; while a soft note is laid
Above the downs. The mysterious land
Spills over from the ridge; and near at hand
Is full of such depth and rich, darker green;
Paths where Man's footprints have but rarely been.
The cattle graze around the lower land;
Content in their haven of shade, they stand.
And amid the green of the hedgerows, trees
Hold in small groups, alone, in twos and threes.
And everywhere one looks, life abounds:
The blackbirds, the pigeons and the sounds
Of finches, beautiful thrushes and more;
And all the life across the downland floor.
Soon these blades will rest; but still for a while;
Grass will then grow in the wake of the mile.
While tailored privet lines the garden side,
And long borders of petalled blossoms hide.
Motionless and alert, a thrush stands near,
Collecting, while calling its young to hear;
To search for their food while they grow and learn
About Nature's world; and then theirs in turn.
The morning sun warms, the dew has risen,
Filmy clouds hang in the pale blue heaven;
While the white upturned moon waits for the hour
To reflect and bathe its hallowed bower,
When all is still, save for the silent flight
Of the whispering forms abroad at night.
The work is done and the meadows of gold
Heighten the shadows which the sun's rays hold
Across these scenes of the most lasting peace;
This landscaped beauty, for us, of our lease.
Nature, time and peace fill this blessed scene;

Purpose of life portraying days between.
This scene is one of radiant beauty;
With the onus on us; for our duty
Is to preserve these scenes: the distant Tor;
The fir forests; the hills; for evermore.
Almost unseen, tiny rivulets fall;
Only by traverse to be seen at all;
Cascading, bubbling down in narrow vales
With magical lustre and fleeting tales
Of enchanted scenes of long boughs that reach,
And slopes of bluebells beneath sprays of beech.
The ash, whose branches plummet to the floor,
Holds poise in its beautiful sheen; no more
To weep alone, but hold the season's height;
Enhance the grandeur of our mortal sight.
The cherry blossomed with a maiden blush,
In the early spring, when the air was fresh;
Then, with the joining of summer and spring,
Laid a pink carpet like a wedding ring.
Union has joined the tressled roses;
They lead to a scene which, rounding, closes.
Here the setting, for centuries, of Man;
Derived of the earth where the world began.
This seat of England, in a setting rare;
Then the sure hand of love became it there.
Yet, the charge of this closing century,
Here and now, standing, must most surely be
To preserve the silhouette and the span;
The recorded scene of history's plan.
Close the thoroughfares to motored power;
And hold this scene forever, a bower
Of men and ages and time caressing;
And parts of history; and of blessings
Found with every tread: of timbered walls
And tiny doorways, arched and tiled and small.
The front of the cathedral, from the green,
Is an enthralling picture to be seen;
Magnificent, impressive pictures are
Now seen from the Tor Woods, high and afar;
Yet, so many fine scenes are to be found
From different points, nearby and around;
Such features from amongst the rooftop files;
And with every visit they beguile

With others: of St Cuthbert's and Priest's Row,
Where the tiny cottages thrill me so.
The Bishop's Eye and open Gateway stand
Joined with Pelleas and Melisande.
The moat, stretching along the palace wall,
Is too beautiful to be real at all.
The ancient Gate House and the Brown's Gate
Combine the setting of time and relate
The importance of guarding these walls, scenes,
Against time's advance; which has never been
So vital . . . Man destroys in a decade
The standings that one thousand years have made.
The glorious West Front, dominating,
Leads through the Penniless Porch, to waiting
Scenes of the market place; the Bishop's Eye.
Still, I think of the names that have gone by.
Time, the fettering measure of our lives,
Becomes eternity as it derives
And transforms: workmen's skills live once again;
Their ways and avenues, now they are lain,
Lead to the pictures we can see, now, here:
Ralph of Shrewsbury, in the greatest fear,
Constructed the moat, the drawbridge and wall
In fear of the townsfolk, lest he should fall;
And Bishop Beckington, who blessed men's feet
With the water that flows down the high street;
The place that was known as the Beggar's Lane,
Where the Ludbrook flowed once its path in vain;
The Almshouses stand repaired and intact;
When I face this scene, I dream, re-enact:
I think of the days when the Ludbrook flowed
And passing history's still changing mode,
Which left here this scene of desolation,
Against a background of preservation.
Still, history has not failed, this, I feel:
Spiders' webs hang on the mantles of steel
And, at morning, the tall fine chimneys stand
To hold these pictures alive and at hand.
But such small pictures, in words, cannot rise
To stories of Jeffries' Bloody Assize;
The City Arms, jail through three hundred years:
The climax of strife until peace grew near;
The museum; the Vicar's Close: the Green;

Not least the cathedral close, to be seen.
Is it where the Sheppey joins with the Brue
That men gave their lives with proud valour true?
And from the Axe to the height of Pen Hill,
Destroying each other in war, until
They joined and Wells became their one prayer:
The cathedral of Wells was centred there.
Succeeding bishops achieved with their stands
Lasting peace, consecration of these lands.
Still these hills reflect Roman history:
Its marks above and around the city;
The long straight paths of men across this land
And their gifts to us of the stones that stand.
The long miles that run from Frome to the sea
Are love's greatest gifts to you and to me.

Michael Larcombe

My First Sonnet

Shall I compare thee to a metronome
That ticks away the time in many ways?
From thy proud birth in such a humble home
'Til now GCSE dissects thy plays.
Rough winds do shake the 'darling buds of May'
We know about this in the twentieth century,
But whereas Will's sonnets last for aye,
The Larkin family's a new discovery.
But thy eternal summer shall not fade,
Many world-over still enjoy thy plays,
The richness of thy language is displayed
In all thy works in countless different ways.
Praise we the bard and long may he be king,
Bring joy and gladness to Man's suffering.

Mary Hinksman

With Thanks

21 today! The publisher announces in his way,
Addressed to my father - now passed away.
His crippled hand no more will write,
The thoughts he penned with failing sight.

But we are grateful you gave the chance,
Willing to give this old man's work a glance.

We were thrilled and so was he,
His works to show in print, you see.
And now we have our lasting memory,
Part of his untold history.

Friends and family gathered at his passing
We sent him on to life e'rlasting.
And yes, it was a privilege for me,
To stand and read his poetry.

Not only published, but spoken,
His words an endearing token,
Of love for his dear wife
Remembered for the whole of life.

What more could I do?
But to convey my thanks to you.
For the shedding of that ray of light,
Upon his fast and fading life.

Reprise:

No great ovation, no trumpets blew
For this man who served in World War II
Four long years he laboured where
Many others would not dare.

Just married he must say farewell
What lay ahead no one could tell.
Bayonets and bullets, deep swampy trench,
Forth as despatch rider he went.

Unknown, unseen, not acknowledged at all,
Silence hid memories and scars he bore.
His pals blown up at his side,
Little keepsake in a drawer he hides.

So many, many unmarked graves,
Men who went to fight with hearts so brave.
Yesterday, Harry, the last to rest,
From World War I, one of the best.

Crowds also line the streets to watch
(Coffins draped in union flag)
The passing of the latest batch,
Of fallen heroes; the nation mourns its dead
Echoes of Harry's words in your head
'No more war,' he said.

Gill Jordan

An Illustration Of A Nearly Man

Eyes to the picture of the soul
The heart don't tell no lies,
Of the crispy crunchy sequence
False composition, a meaning in disguise.

What feeling of the movement and the manners
Of how to look at what you see,
A hungry face but with diamond teardrops
Reminisce of how it could be.

An illustration of a nearly man
An antagonist or a protagonist,
You can never tell on reflection
Of an evil mind but with good intentions.

Michael Avery

Nature's Gift

When we fly in the sky
When we meet the clouds
That covers us from above
The clouds are like marshmallows
The air is so clear
As you peer down onto the land
The sighting of the fields
Give a warm feeling like a quilt
The further you rise into the skies
The closer you get to the heavens
Life in the sky is such a breeze
Life as a bird is so peaceful
Only for a little while
All the nice sceneries
Of our beaches and seas
They mustn't be forgotten
Our many fields that can go forever
Must not be trod on
The birds that use the sky as a playground
One day it *may n*ot be there
Let's let them play and fly
We need to keep the air clean
Nature should always be there to be seen in the sky
The quilt of our land need to look after
We don't want to see it disappear
Nature *was* a wonderful thing
As progress was to be made by mankind
As the years went by
As the birds want to continue to fly.

Robert Bradley

Bipolar

'Where are you going, my beautiful girl?
Is your mind on a journey where we cannot go?
Does your heart feel it's breaking . . . or is it aglow?
Drifting along with your head in a whirl,
Beautiful, beautiful, beautiful girl.'

'Beautiful girl keep your feet on the ground.
Are you dancing with sunbeams this glorious day,
Or off with the fairies where fantasies play
And witches and warlocks and dragons abound?
Where we cannot reach you, where you can't be found.'

'Of what are you dreaming, my beautiful one?
Are you up on a cloud with your eyes full of stars,
Are you floating past Neptune and Venus and Mars?
Does the Milky Way beckon you on from the sun?
Beautiful, beautiful, beautiful one.'

'Oh beautiful girl, do your demons seem real?
When darkness descends and bad dreams fill your sleep,
Do suspicions and thoughts that are black start to creep
Into your head and your peace of mind steal?
Filling the night hours with pictures surreal?'

'Why are you crying, my beautiful girl?
Does your bleak world seem empty of hope and true love?
Try lifting your eyes to the stars up above;
The world is your oyster, inside is the pearl!
My beautiful, beautiful, beautiful girl.'

Yvonne Lane

My Dad

My dad was a soldier
He meant a lot to me
He used to tell me stories
As he sat me on his knee

One day he went away to war
To me it seemed like years
I thought about him every night
As I wiped away the tears

He wrote to Mum and told her
He wished he was at home
He misses all his comforts
Like being home alone

They teach you how to shoot to kill
I really don't want to know
I try to hide my feelings
It really hurts me so

It wasn't long before we heard
My dad was sent away
To fight with all his comrades
Well, 'What could he say?'

Time went on, we did not hear
Our thoughts began to stray
There did not seem any reason
Why we had not heard that day

But on that Christmas morning
A telegram arrived
I would not see my dad again
Because I knew he died.

I cried myself to sleep that night
And thought of what he'd said
My dad meant a lot to me
And now of course he's dead

That is what you get you see
When off you go to war
Leaving all your loved ones
And seeing them no more

Let's hope that in the future
There will be no more wars
Where people will live together
And time will take its course

Let's hope that my old dad
Did not lose his life in vain
And that all I have been through
Cannot happen again.

G B Little

Heaven Scent!

Over the heath and down the dale,
In the misty, murky, chilly dawn,
Fox runs urgently, tired and fraught.
He must find shelter or be caught;
Betrayed by a glimpse of his tail!

Down in the undergrowth, under the guns,
There, in the copse where the woodcock flies;
His delicate ears can hear those sounds -
The hunting cry and the baying hounds
So now, for his life, he runs.

Pale sunlight glints in his terrified eyes
As, wildly he dashes through bracken and broom,
Then across fields ploughed fresh for the corn
Pursued by that strident hunting horn;
Could this be the day that he dies?

But, no need to run now, no need to worry;
The hounds no longer continue the chase,
For fox it seems, in his panic flight
Had, quite by chance and in his fright,
Dashed through a field of slurry!

J Unsworth

The Keepsake

Yesterday came the man from the hospice in his van
to collect my dear, dead darling's clothes . . .
all that made him what he was;
his knife sharp suits, proud badged blazers,
mirror shone shoes - ah, but he was an immaculate man,
tall and elegant.
But now, as I see the empty drawers and hangers
swinging useless on the rail, I feel bereft,
as though he had just died.
One thing is left . . . I kept his evening bow tie.
Not for him the clip-on, made-up article.
He would stand before me, handsome in his evening suit,
chin raised so that I could tie his tie into a neat black bow.
Then he would kiss me lightly and we'd go
to whatever function we'd been titivating for.
If there was dancing he would whirl me round the floor,
like Fred and Ginger, to a waltz or quickstep before
the hoppers and jiggers brought us to a halt and we would retire
breathless to our table and our g and ts.
Now, as I run its silken softness through my fingers,
remembering our life together, year by year,
I see him standing, chin held up,
smiling whilst I tie his tie into a neat black bow
and I know that all that made him is still here.

Vera Burrell

War And Peace

This world was safe in my childhood years,
We all played outside without any fear.
Went for bike rides, cycled for miles,
Walked through open fields and over stiles.
Those initial years just after the war,
How could we have envisaged what was in store.
Everything was on ration in those days,
And folk worked hard for so little pay.
Coupons for clothes and coupons for sweets,
Without those coupons there were no treats.
Money was short we were now at peace,
That horrific war had now ceased.
Over fifty years on this world's in a terrible state,
Bombings and killings - it's now filled with hate.
Youngsters boozing and taking drugs,
People battling cancer and horrid superbugs.
Our young soldiers dying on distant shores,
All these years later and we're still at war.

Zoiyar Cole

Thoughts In A Garden

A gardener's job must be the best,
more satisfying than all the rest.
Working towards that perfect bloom
with added prize, a sweet perfume.

Alongside nature's open door,
attuned with insects, birds and more.
From seeds and bulbs and cuttings too,
a true fulfilment, something new.

Nurturing, loving, all consuming;
a passion that is non-assuming.
A sigh reflecting pleasure found,
and here is peace, that perfect sound.

Some colours blend and others blaze.
Mix emotions, calm, amaze.
The structures, vistas, all sublime
just like a vision made to rhyme.

A favourite flower, or shrub or tree,
we all are individuals free
with wondrous choice, amazingly
from hybrid rose to wild daisy

And here the rat race far away,
there's time to think and even pray.
From window box to grand estate,
there'll be a flower to contemplate.

Jo Robson

Sunset And Dreams

I am really sure I saw them beneath the gnarled old oak,
I've often read about them, the little elfin folk,
They flittered here, they flittered there,
They came and danced quite near my chair,
I blinked my eyes and shook my head,
Um? It's really time I went to bed.

Doreen Christopher

Forrard

Forward implies progress,
Improvement, evolution and continuity;
A coming of age
For the Press.

Some would say,
It is all vanity,
But then,
No poet has the monopoly on this.

We all wish to be heard,
In our own way,
We choose our words,
And have our say.

We mine them,
Move them about the page.
They can be comic, sad or sage.

Eventually, they settle,
Into a work,
Now we can *pop* the champagne cork!

Vivienne Wachenje

Phoenix

So colourful, my cockatiel
He's orange white and yellow
Was just a baby when he came -
Now he's a 'cocky' yellow fellow!

Hand-reared especially for me
And hatched in spring 09 -
A great companion he's become
He whistles, talks and climbs

Around the living room he flies
Each morning when I clean
His lovely cage I call his house -
Then he sits on me to preen!

I've named him Phoenix as it seems
He's risen from the ashes!
For at this time his tail is grey
And he's moulting - so bare patches!

He's easy to feed as greens are his choice,
An assortment of seeds are a boon
His hearing's acute and he's very astute
When out to play in the afternoon!

This very small bird so cute and so bright
Copies my whistled tune
It gives us great pleasure making music together
He's brightened my life - no more gloom!

Pam Dutton

Pastoral

I sat before an old inn door
To sup my ale, and pause awhile.
The rusty smock I proudly wore
Was rent with age and out of style,
But underneath my ancient gown
My heart was happy, free of care
For me no bustling of the town,
But time to think, and time to spare.

The air sweet fresh from passing rain
Hung heavy with a soft soil smell,
Tomorrow I would sow my grain
But now I'd time to rest a spell,
To drink and chew and look awhile
Or nod my head to passers-by,
To friends I'd give a cheery smile
While maidens such a wink and sigh.

Daylight fades now into dusk
And so I start upon my way,
Spitting out a golden husk,
While with the passing of the day
The cottage windows glow with light.
The dew lies heavy in the air
As bats awaken with the night
While I'm so happy, free of care.

Sheila Benard

Safe

Sleep - at last
Safety - at last
Peace - at the last

going to interface
between
sleeping and waking
life and
the further life

time
yields an appointed time
my
passing will be
a quest

into
other reality
good
I can sleep
in safety
window open

skin
soft breeze
anointing
my
waiting body
then waking

each
gull anthemed
morning
seeing time
coming
when angel loved ones

ferry
my soul,
my true self
beyond
the horizon
ever closer

than breathing

Mum, Dad
Grannie, Grandad
Richard
my
brother

all loved
ones live
differently
no
real
separation

my death
is the journey out
I long for
sleep finding
deeper awakening
in the one life

The appointed
time waits as a wise
one,
companion in
the valley of
shadow

here
where the pilgrim
soul
journeys sharing
treasures
from its

path
where, on the
crossroads
showing
the paths from
endless shadow
a child
innocent, lost
runs screaming, cast out
by
evil in many forms

life
whole life
entry into
one life
of the created
order

needs
innocence, needs
the wise one
holding
the cord of love
linking

to beyond
the horizon
where
like a waiting
treasure is
the divine abiding

my lady
of silence be
the source
of all we share
one creation
reaches out

like a
yearning
tree
for no sound
only
that beyond
human hearing

my lady
of silence loose
all shackles
of ignorance,
of fear
restore

humanity
broken like glass
yet in

each piece
wantonly discarded
find again the true light

take us
to freedom
loosed from the
great evil
the predatory
silence of friends.

George Coombs

Like A Patient Cultivating A Cancer

I'd lost my head,
clearly I had gone mad with need,
for a new personality, a new body to feel.
I shined with lust that seeped from the pores,
my head salivated with my times faces
and my lungs inflated with an exotic air.
I travelled to different people like the light -
Incandescent.
And I sat in the dark consequence and pretended
all was as it should be, I was the performer
at every soiree; always one eye on the door.
I leant upon the strange notions every day,
and drank to better see me through them;
imbibed, inhaled, injected
way along the road of disillusionment.
This abysmal darkness that is only alleviated
through total intoxication of the senses,
through slow disintegration of the brain,
where was my spirit?

Jason Russell

Born Bad

Born bad
Through and through
Born bad
And beautiful
That's you
I can't stop loving you
Though people say
I'm insane
That you're only after my money
That loving me
Is just your silly game
Born bad
Through and through
Born bad
That's you
You said you were having my baby
You blackmailed me over it
Drove me crazy
So I did the right thing
And married you
Gave you diamonds
And a wedding ring
Gave you your heart's desire
Because you set my heart on fire
I did what you wanted
Thinking you'd be loyal and true
When my back was turned
I found you
With somebody new
In came this guy
Much richer and more famous
Than I
your away with him
My love for you
Doesn't see the light of day
You've taken him now
As your lover
Declaring to him
There'll be no other
Just like you did with me

But I'll take you back
Don't you see
If you were to return
My darling to me
For I love you too deeply
To give you up
Although you're bad
Just like a naughty pup
You're much worse than that
You were born bad
Through and through
Born bad
And beautiful
That's you.

Barbara Towes

Untitled

These fickle humans I don't understand.
They're surely placed on Earth us birds to feed.
Some days they have us feeding from their hand,
Yet next day seem oblivious of our need.
This summer morning I was up at dawn,
With chirruping my feeders to awake
Yet on they slept, and left we birds to mourn,
The fact we'd failed their feelings to elate.
The blackbird's sweetest notes have gone unheard.
The thrush's throat with singing now is sore.
Pigeons and sparrows - every kind of bird,
Stand motionless, and hungry, at each door.
    Surely they see we lead a life of woe.
    How then can they transgress, and treat us so?

A W Ansell

Magic Season

The evening,
      Is damp,
And sleet, rain, so softly falling all around.
The street lamps,
All aglow, shine down on the people below.
Umbrellas held high, that once matched the rainbow in the sky.
There is a whisper in the breeze,
That the magic season will soon begin.
The church bells ring out loud and clear,
      For Jesus Christ,
           Our Saviour is near.

Iris Davey

Twenty-One Years On

I was at the time beginning,
With the aim of really winning.
To get my verse read,
So maybe a way earning bread.

How twenty-one years have flown by,
All this time I might try.
To get publisher to print my book,
For so many hours it has took.

It is something I really enjoy
For I have written since a boy.
So it's had its compensation,
At my attempts at recitation.

May I offer my congratulation?
You have done for poets across the nation.
There is so many now,
To get to top somehow.

Would be so good to write a masterpiece,
But even then I would not cease.
Although I have covered much ground,
It keeps my mind and really sound.

R E J Gent

Cruel Sport

In the clouds' mist
Shadows in the sky
Proud and majestic
Two eagles fly

In easy circles
The flight goes yonder
Spellbound I watch
Eyes filled with wonder

Wind gently sings
Dusk is just about to fall
Silence is broken
By the eagles' call

A sudden blast
Like thunder!
Blood! A broken wing!
A loud cry of pain
A fall in the wind . . . !

One eagle only
Remains in sight
Flapping her wings
In melancholic flight
The wind is repeating
Her cry of hate!
The mist's a shroud
For her ravaged mate . . . !

Vaifro Malavolta

A Glimpse Of Hell

How can I look into your eyes, and tell you that I will always keep you safe,
When you have had a glimpse of Hell, and I could not be there with you?
Though my soul shared every anguished moment, there was nothing I could do.
The pain of hearing gunshots, not knowing who or what the bullets pierced.
How could I *not* hope that it was someone else's child or relative who died?
A hope invoked by desperation, and it could not be denied.
I felt so ashamed and guilty, of praying 'Not my child please'
We all came to the school to celebrate the beginning of another term,
But you were all taught something of life that you were never meant to learn.
Being held as hostages, while the whole world watched and held its breath.
I was somewhere else, while you and your mother went to the school alone.
And by the time that I arrived, the seeds of terror were already sown.
I stood with the others whose loved ones were imprisoned in those walls.
Saying prayers for our children's safety, and for brothers, sisters and wives.
Trying to make sense of the nightmare that had taken over all our lives.
Fathers, mothers, grans and grandads, aunts and uncles and cousins too.
This was meant to be a real 'fun' day, a celebration for the young and old,
Instead we stood and watched that terrible scenario unfold.
We heard explosions, we saw smoke and flames, we saw unforgettable sights.
People shot as they ran away from the collapsed, and burning gym.
Where many more were left dead or dying, shot or stabbed at a captor's whim.
The air was filled with the stench of death, of smoke, and the smell of fear.
I tried to find an answer to the question all were asking, why, tell us why,
Tell us the reason why our children and our relatives had to die?
What cause could be so great that innocents had to pay for it with their lives?
The soldiers stormed the building when it seemed there was no other way.
Though many will question what history will write about that wretched day.
My poor child, what horrors have your eyes beheld, what sounds assailed your
ears?
I don't know how I can tell you about your mother, sadly, she lost her life.
We have both lost someone, you your devoted mother, and I my loving wife.
They brought so many bodies out; a seemingly never-ending trail of grief.
I could hardly see your face, my eyes were blurred with the tears I'd shed.
But oh the joy and happiness when I realised that you weren't also dead.
No one will ever forget the sights of injured men and women, or the children.
Limbs twisted and torn, and body parts scattered everywhere.
A tiny girl lying where she fell, her red blood dimming the gold of her hair.
While a young boy lies beside her, his arm, even in death trying to shield her.
So many graves to be dug, and so many mourners to give their sorrow voice.
More than three hundred souls for whom life or death was not a choice.

Some of those who perpetrated this immense and evil crime,
Died by their own, or by a Russian soldier's unforgiving hand.
While the people struggle with their grief, and call for vengeance in their land.
And again I ask how can I look into your eyes my child, and not see reflected there
All the horrors you have seen, and still say to you that I will always
Keep you safe, and protect you from all the mem'ries that will forever haunt your
days.

B M Buckle

Lucky Beer (Bognor Regis Pier)

Must be the country's shortest pier
Nevertheless it has all the mechanical gear
Slot machines all around
Coins clattering down
Might make a mint
Get the hint
But winning or skint
Time for a beer
At the Alex, a good pub, quite near
Bognor Regis by the sea
Happy days mostly for free
Quite the place for you and me
One of the prettier places to see
Shangri La quite near, not far
All you need is the train, bus or a car.

Barry Dillon

The Sun King

The trilling linnet heralds dawn,
Sweet gentle flowers spring,
To greet their noble master
Their shining rightful king.
Sunflowers turn their gaze on him
Cornflowers sway their heads,
Even tiny weeds salute him
From humble dandelion beds.
Mighty trees stand to attention
Limbs outstretched to meet the day,
Offering shelter and protection
To all who chance upon their way.
Mother Nature tends her children
Knowing well 'ere the sun is high,
Though all around, life is beginning,
Still John Barleycorn must die.
Soon enough, the pearly moon shall
Show his face, and take his turn,
Watching o'er all God's good children,
Who await his brother, Sun's return.

David Duncan

The Letter

I wrote my love a letter, intending to upset her,
Telling her she could not be my bride;
And the letter that I sent was full of argument
And, oh, how my darling cried!

Each line is well rehearsed, precise and not perverse,
Saying she is not what I admire;
But these words I came to rue for they truly were not true,
And branded me as no more than a liar.

Once many words were mentioned to put me in contention -
Number one in favour with her heart;
But the impression that I made was only second grade,
And silently she said I should depart.

So I thought how to annoy her, to totally destroy her
For humiliating me in such a way;
So I took hold of a pen, some ink and paper then
I wrote to her the words I had to say.

I sent her such a sentence which spoke of no repentance,
Saying she is not what I require;
Yet my love will never yield and this letter is a shield,
For truly she is still my heart's desire.

Keith Trutzenbach

Reggie

I am a cat named Reggie;
My coat is grey with stripes.
I look like a tiger
Prowling in the night.

I have a favourite chair
In which to lay my head.
I like to claw and scratch it,
Because I think it is a bed.

I love my mum to call me
Because I love my fish.
I find it very tasty,
With biscuits in my dish.

At night I sleep upon the chair
Dreaming of the mice.
My mum says that I mustn't hurt them
It isn't very nice.

My half-brother's name is Sooty.
I chase him through the house.
But he taught me a lesson
By pinching my mouse.

I don't mean to be a bully;
I think it is great fun.
But if I do it too often,
I get told off by my mum.

L Roberts

Sir Ronald Reagan

Valiant talented man is he
Who became a film actor on TV
His sanguine spirit rose for more
He played his part in the Second World War.

He took up jogging, immense fun to be
Got carried away and ran for presidency
Obviously he ran his race hell-bent
Then became the American President.

His laughter and mannerisms we have seen
Brought him to England to visit the Queen
Being the President was quite a stir
He went a bit further and became a 'Sir'.

Sir Ronald Reagan is his name
The American actor that played the game
Sadly when the final curtain fell the world cried,
To be told 'Sir' Ronald Reagan had died . . .

Diane Full

Summer Holidays 24/7/2001

The summer holidays are here again
Six weeks of mayhem
Off to the beach, park, amusements and all
Going on rides that go up and down
Round and round, you get so dizzy you could fall
Playing in the sand, and swimming in the sea
Hey Mum, Dad, take a photo of me
Jumping in and out of the waves
That's fun for me.
Mum and Dad just sit on the beach
They go so red they look like a ripened peach
Eating ice cream, fish and chips
With salt and vinegar and gritty bits
Oh that sand gets everywhere.
It's now the evening, time to go home
We all fall asleep in the car
But Dad has to stay awake, he has to drive far
When we get home we go to bed
Knackered and tired, I've been excited
And my belly's fed.
Goodnight all.

David Skinner

The Shelter

Fears turn to tears, but not for long,
Before you know it, they are all gone,
Don't be afraid by darkness in the night,
By the morning it turns into a bright shining light.

Whatever seems big now, will soon fade away,
Whatever seems strong, gets weaker each day,
As quick as a cloud passes in a storm,
So does the worries that make you look worn.

God can give you love, hope, joy and peace,
God shelters all those who want hurting to cease,
He will never leave you, forever He is,
Eternal and loving, watching the sheep who are His.

God's love is a tower, keeping you near,
God's love is a refuge, He won't miss a tear.
Whatever your heartache, whomever's hurt you,
He's waiting and hoping, you'll let Him love you.

Kim Solomons

Love

Wonderful to know you
	Someone to talk to
Understanding each other
	In everything we do
We give love to each other
It could happen to you.
	Falling in love
The great romantic
	Is us.

Julie May Wiles

Sunny Times

Where have the summers gone,
Of when the child I was and dreams I remember.
Running in the fields with my brother and sisters,
Mother coming up behind
Father working on the farm.
How happy I was then in my little world.
Poppies, deep red poppies growing in the corn.
The warm summer sun warm on our faces.
Laughter in full bloom
A picnic spread on grass of green at noon.
Cold drinks of squash, jam sandwiches, biscuits and cake.
Games we played of hide-and-seek.
Summer days, how they did fly
Like the bird and the butterfly.
Was it really so long ago?

S J Orgill

Boots On The Ground

Boots on the ground,
More boots on the ground.
The word had gone round,
We need boots on the ground.

Afghanistan bound
Putting boots on the ground,
The logic was sound
For more boots on the ground.

Yet explosives abound
Lifting boots off the ground
And little was found
Of their boots on the ground.

Now bugles will sound
To mourn boots on the ground,
We hear no more sound
From their boots underground.

Michael Shannon

Such Times As These

(For my mother Vera Kitchenham, 1915-2009)

'There never were such times as these,'
She said,

And as she spoke,
I thought,

There is the truth of it -

Never were there such times as these,
Never one part pre-perceived,

Or one more valuable than another:
As to the child, so to the mother.

And as she spoke,
I caught

A glimpse of grey skies burst apart
Revealing a fierce spring blue to lift the heart;

Revealing a new start

About to begin - and never were we in

Such times as these.

Sarah Wright

The Men From Mullion

In memory does my mind meander back to Kernow's coast once more,
And through the high-banked lanes I wander down to the grey inn by the shore.
T'was there, mid pints of ale a-flowing, were sung the Cornish songs of yore.

    I see the harbour lights a-waking,
    Across Mount's Bay the grey seas breaking,
    While melodious from the inn a-ringing
    I hear the men from Mullion singing.

Before the open fire I'm seated, free once more from storm and care.
In Fishing Cove the wild waves thunder. Here the 'White Rose', soft and fair,
And, 'Lead me, Oh Thou Great Jehova' like an organ fills the air.

    Outside, the harbour lights are waking.
    Across Mount's Bay the grey seas breaking,
    While melodious in the inn a-ringing
    I join the men from Mullion singing.

'Oh, Let the Harbour Lights Keep Burning'. Our lads are safe from tempest's might
And drink and sing, but still are mindful (Lord help the sailor on this night).
Coast-wise Cornishmen still singing, 'Lead Us To Thy Heavenly Light'.

    And still the harbour lights are flashing.
    Across Mount's Bay the grey seas crashing,
    While melodious in the inn a-ringing
    Are Cornishmen from Mullion singing.

But now Trelawney's heard not often in the grey inn by the shore.
Is 'Camborne Hill' to be forgotten? The 'Robber's Song' is heard no more.
But back-along, in happy dreaming, we sing those Cornish songs of yore.

    In Cornwall, harbour lights are waking.
    Across Mount's bay the grey seas breaking.
    Oh, Lord, once more to hear the ringing
    Of gentlemen from Mullion singing.

Peter A Green

A Great Decision

We at the Medway Towns have been struck a heavy blow,
We are to lose one of our dignitaries, that is regretfully so.
We have been informed by the press, by wireless and television,
We are to lose a great man of statue and vision.

The Bishop of Rochester, Dr Michael Nazir Ali has made a decision of import,
He feels passionately his energies elsewhere are sought.
He wishes to devote his time in helping the persecuted Christians in Pakistan and
Iran,
To give them support, encouragement and make conversions where he can.

The Bishop's opinions and views are listened to with care,
He will voice his thoughts where others should, but do not dare.
He is a great Christian and wants the entire world to be Christians too,
He would like to coerce the non-believers to see his point of view.

He is prepared to give up high office, its privileges and grace,
To go into the wilderness and meet non-Christians face to face.
With his determination, charisma, courage and charm,
He wants everyone to enjoy the care of being in the cradle of God's loving arms.

In his high office as bishop he has received many a death threat,
Because others don't like the uncomfortable truths which upset.
He greets you with a smile and enchants you with his quiet persuasive way,
You regret when he has left you, you then realise you wanted him to stay.

Whatever your persuasion, you know a man like this is hard to find,
Who makes such a personal sacrifice to win over the unbelievers of mankind.
The world is an ever changing place, for good or bad,
The loss of our dear Bishop will make many others needing his comfort glad.

Dear Michael, Bishop of Rochester, with full hearts we wish you well,
And pray the Good Lord will be with you and help
To bring much happiness to those who come under your spell.

Terry Godwin

Seaford River

Our house stands on the old riverbed
Once an area of historic seapower
Ships sailed out - so gallantly led
Giving Drake's men their finest hour

Blessed with the wind and the tide
The Armada outgunned and dismayed
Blown off course and nowhere to hide
Spanish might, a sorry sight portrayed

Ships came from distant lands
Some from far across the Equator
Imagine where our house now stands
If viewed from window as spectator

Unloading their cargoes onto wharfside
Rolling out on the quay wine casks
All manner of cargoes awaiting the tide
Sea shanties sang along in their tasks

One thinks of tough seafaring folk
Ship's cannon to ward off invaders
Ships so sturdily built of oak
Crews not dressed as present day sailors

River entrance now long past
When river mouth began to silt up
Much of the area now is grassed
With a road of houses built-up.

Sea captains sought refuge in this river
History of wreckers' lights from the shore
What hazards with cargoes to deliver
All those ships and seafarers no more.

Len Peach

Invitation To Kent

Discover our precious lanes, woodlands and byways
Where a day can enfold heritage, history, hobbies,
Smugglers' tales, so tactile and true!
Villages celebrating summer days too,
Veteran cars, flower festivals, open gardens, craft and art shows.
Our Wealden panorama simply is stunning,
The North Downs and Pilgrims' Way to explore,
Trace our royal history, Napoleon and more!
Coastal 'gems' and Romney Marsh secrets,
A sense of tradition at every turn.
Castles, cathedrals, cottages, concerts and 'gigs'.
See a country wedding, bells ringing joyously
No matter how late the bride's arrival!
Cricket on the green
Always a pleasure to be seen,
Bangers and mash, cream teas
And a wide choice of hot meals to please.
Simply celebrate and have fun,
Activities, scenery and a brilliant sun!

Margaret Ann Wheatley

Loving You

I love you today
As I loved you yesterday
But the situations of yesterday
Are still here today

In my dreams it is yesterday
And I pretend it is today
But when morning comes and dreams fade
Once more I am alone

So I will lock you away in my heart
Until this love of yesterday
Can once more be the love of today
For all the tomorrows when we can be as one.

Linda E Carter

Destiny

An icy hand clutches
daily,
Earth's crushing dark engulfs
choking
I know my destiny
Early death
yet, hard I fight
oblivion holds no promise
Illnesses have weakened
unrelenting pain, worn
medicines failed
Still, I wish for life
each day now
doctors administer poisonous balm
minister, relatives, friends, stay near
loving hands caress
beloved voices echo
I hear, keening for the dead
For me!
Struggle lost.

June Fox

Untitled

A book to read, a hand to hold
A smile when a loved one draws near
Warmth of a fire, a pet on the mat
Life is worthwhile, no need to chat
Your mind is lost in the wonder of words
There are thin books, fat books
Open the pages, the words will enthral
And bring pictures to your mind
Some words make you smile
Some make you cry
But the meaning of words
Make life worthwhile.

Joan M Waller

The Dungeness Lifeboat Crew

Dungeness, a lonely, windswept isolated place
Presents to the world such a desolate face
Brave-hearted men its one saving grace
Heroes one and all.

Mother Nature, may do her worst
Heavens open, floodgates burst
Men at sea by Neptune cursed
Brave men answer their call.

Personal worries they selflessly hide
As they don their uniform with a sense of pride
Professional, labourer side by side
Not knowing what may befall.

Volunteers all, their pockets unlined
Working only for the good of mankind
Braver men you may never find
Dungeness men stand tall.

You deserve our thanks, yet you ask for none
Happy to be home safe when your work is done
Ready once more should another call come
Heroes one and all.

Christine Collins

One With You

The balance of justice,
May never swing true,
At times like these,
They will look to you.

Are you ready to take up the calling?
Are you ready to be one?
You are someone's daughter,
You are someone's son.

I wonder if they ever knew,
What you would become,
Now it is you,
Who knows what must be done.

Take up your place,
In the defence against crime,
Be steadfast, strong and true.

The balance of justice,
May never swing true,
Shoulder to shoulder we stand,
We are many they are few.

For you are one of us now,
And we are one with you.

Graham Newman

Anthropology

So God created man in his own image, in the image of God created he him;
male and female created he them'. Genesis 1:27

Creation's six long days elapsed;
    The firsts of life appeared:
Each man and beast and living thing
    Created whole, not reared.

Yet science, strangely, seems to think
    That, somewhere in the gloom,
Infinitesimal fluxions did
    Enable life to bloom
When everything is breathed by God.
    Now Adam, from the dust,
And Eva, from his rib, brought shame,
    For they'd betrayed God's trust.

Then graceful Noah and his kin,
    The violent world unspared,
Began with God a whole new world -
    Yet still by sin impaired.

So Jesus came, the Saviour,
    His flesh and blood to give,
That we, partaking, should know love,
    That, through it, we might live.

For God intended us to do
    Whatever we do best -
Some do it well and others try
    Before we're laid to rest.

Death's vice-like grip will be appeased
    When we, in shrouded place,
Awaken to the call of Christ -
    Then see God face to face.

John Goulding

Autumn Walk

When the leaves are whirling landwards
And the sky is blue, not black,
Breathing air that's like champagne,
We're setting out along the track
That will lead us to the village
On this sparkling autumn morn,
Passing hedges bright with berries,
Rose fruits, bramble and hawthorn
Entwined with the wild clematis -
Travellers' joy or old man's beard -
And spiders' webs are shimmering,
Then the robin's voice is heard,
From the top branch of an ash tree
He is carolling to the sky,
A reminder of the summer
To these walkers passing by.

Feet shuffling through the leaves
That are carpetting the lane
And the scent of autumn rising
From those rotting down from rain.
Cleared of bounty from the harvest
The fields beside are lying bare
A haven for golden pheasants
That are gleaning them with care.
A tractor on the horizon
Begins the cycle once again
As it ploughs that rich brown earth
To receive the next year's grain.
Seagulls are swirling behind it
Enjoying the sudden feast
Which overturning of the clods
Has so rapidly released.

Now the village is appearing
With its cottages, neat and trim,
Little gardens, well-attended,
Filled with flowers to the brim,
Chrysanthemums red and golden,
Late geraniums mauve and white,
Fuchsia, cyclamens, sedum,
A bright and welcoming sight.

Fiery creepers paint the walls
Of this pleasing neighbourhood
As smoke spirals from the chimneys
With a lingering scent of wood.
At an ancient country inn
We are pausing for a while
To enjoy their food and drink
Served to us with a smile.

Then it is on passed church and school
And the children running round
With shouts of joyful laughter
As they circulate the ground.
The sky is clouding over,
And the wind begins to rise,
Evening approaches swiftly
Darkening before our eyes.
Now rooks are heading homewards
At the ending of this day,
We too must retrace our footsteps
In a tired but happy way.
We are heeding the call of home
As we hurry through the lane.
This day, an autumn treasure,
In our memories will remain.

J Jill Garner

The Nature Trail

Here beneath the trees
Upon a windless breeze
Hearts held at ease
On a shifting sigh
And then a laugh
Coarse, breathless, harsh
A chorus of chattering leaves
A smoky owl slightly
Lights upon a leafy bough
His light perch drifts
As snow-white swans
Dive to watery deeps
Gunpowder at Oare
Now a walkway with nature
These marine drenched wastes
Aliven one's soul.

R J Collins

A Sonnet

Octet
Let's write a sonnet
only fourteen lines
what shall I write about?
Not the Spring and not the downs
How about jazz or fairy rings?
Theosophy or medieval kings?
Just two more lines
to complete the octet

Sectet
Let my pen glide
and enjoy the ride
let the words slide
the joy of play in
the composing of
a sonnet.

Elizabeth T Jenks

Beaches

'Tis Christmas Day in Whitley Bay,
The sands are clean as a whistle,
Our beachcomber club met today
To dine at the Dog and Thistle.

Turkey and Christmas pud aren't here,
They much prefer lobster and crab,
And wash it down with local beer
Along with fat willicks and dab.

Billy Boy said to Nancy Morgan
I'm so glad that you came along.
I've brought my electric organ,
I hope you can give us a song.

Jackie Green told big Mary Hood
She could play with his detector.
Mary thought he was downright rude
So she rang the local inspector!

Shifty Sam put his arm round Sue,
Your red and white wellies are sweet.
Don't think I'm mean, if I tell you
You got them on the wrong feet!

Bert Black gave them plenty of crack,
This shovel is twenty years old.
Only three new spades going back
And seven new handles I'm told!

They walked on the sand, raked out some stone
So the starlight dancing could start.
Big Malone was a star on his own
When he rocked Red Ruby apart!

So praise them all when summer breaks,
The new year is not far away.
Polished shovels and sharpened rakes,
They'll be cleaning our beach every day!

Alan Dee

Daisy, Daisy, Poor, Poor Daisy!

Lazy Daisy felt rather hazy
After a drop of Scotch!
So she sat on a chair
That wasn't there!
But it didn't worry her much.
She counted her fingers
And then her toes
To make sure she had all of them.
But she wasn't sure,
So she counted once more
And stopped when she got to ten!
So she tried again just to get it right.
Poor Daisy! Poor Daisy!
Who was ever so tight.
She tried to stand up
But found she was stuck
For she'd sat on a tin of glue!
And should you see Daisy who is still rather hazy
With a tin of glue on her posterior
Don't give her a miss
Just give her a kiss
For she's feeling rather inferior!
And wouldn't you if you had sat on a tin of glue?
Well! think of poor Daisy who's still very hazy
And wandering o'er hill and dale
Feeling forlorn and ever so worn
And of course, looking extremely pale
So the lesson to learn, is do not yearn
For a drop of Scotch or maybe more
Or you'll end up hazy
Perhaps slightly crazy and just like Daisy
That's for sure!

R Bateman

Alava Dawn

Awake with a yawn, outside awaiting me
An Alava dawn. In the quiet morn thank
God I was born. In their warm beds
Fast asleep dream scenes sleepers keep.
The silent world is mine and all that's in it.
And so my joy knows no limit.
I am in tune with the infinite, at one with
Nature and all her glory. Overhead an eagle
Soars, while homeward flies the night owl
While all the time sleepers, to bed-keepers snore.
For I am bound for a secret lake, careful of the
Route I take, unwilling the serene scene to share,
Of limpid waters mist garbed with soft twisting
Spectral, spirals ascending, thinking Nature's gifts are
Unending. There in the tranquil centre floats in mid-air, a spectral
Statuesque figure made of ethereal stuff I swear!
Motionless, epitomy of awaredness, a solitary sentinel suddenly
Into life galvanised, its long beak with lightning action,
Spears a fish for its breakfast satisfaction.
Sometime soon it will fly away as it has another
Part to play, together with a constant mate will
A heronry create, and thus will arise a new generation,
To excite in me a warm sensation.
And so those heavy sleepers have my pity,
Since no such rewards are found in town or city.

Graham Watkins

The Waverley

Gangplank down,
Crowds surging forward.
Tickets flapping in the gale.
Whoops! there mine goes.

With a boom and a splutter
She sails into frosty, salty air
Chugging past the Sussex coast,
Waterproofs and cameras at the ready.

As I gaze out the porthole,
Sea pounding and churning below,
Desperately searching for a puffin,
A voice beside me says, 'Do you come here often?'

We chatted away happily,
Spray touching our rosy cheeks,
Cameras and binoculars at the ready
But no brandy smugglers in sight.

Gangplank lifted down,
Safe at last.
'Can I see you again?' he asked.
The wind tugging at my woolly hat.
'Of course!'

Sarah Diskin

Great British Holidays

Tap water we can drink,
There's no need to suffer jabs,
Of different tongues we don't think,
There's clean water in our lavs.

Countryside all lush and green,
While the sea is clear and blue,
No mosquitoes to be seen,
A warm welcome's here for you.

Passport, visa, we can forget,
No delay or wait for plane,
Stay near home you won't regret
Your choice, it won't be in vain.

Shellfish and food we eat,
No stomach upsets dog you,
Never tied to toilet seat,
No travel agents you need sue.

No hot sun to burn your skin,
Just warm but never too hot,
Here you've tonic with your gin,
Just enjoy yourselves a lot.

Papers, post and phone all near,
If you need to keep in touch,
You'll holiday without fear
And enjoy yourselves so much.

Suzanne J Golding

The Dangerous Bath Seat

*(Upon discharge from hospital, my wife received several visits from the nurses of 'The Early Discharge Team'.
A group of nurses who supply you with such things as bath seats and toilet arm rests. I dedicate this to one of
them, a nurse named Sarah, a rather shy young lady.)*

I answered the door, and Sarah was there,
That charming nurse, who had last brought a chair.
She now brought a bath seat, for us both to share,
As we are aged, and have to take care.

She kindly fitted it up, and explained it all.
Showed how to use it, with me in the hall.
Told the wife how to sit, and how never to fall
Clever young woman, like being at school.

Then to me she said, 'Watch your follicles Sir,
When you're sitting on the seat.'
For a bit of fun, I queried her,
Asking, 'Do you mean my feet?'

But no, she was very mystical,
As she looked slightly red in the face,
Or maybe she was diplomatical,
But she then spoke with very good grace.

She referred to my 'follicles' as 'articles'
And started all over again,
And in a musical way, quite dramatical,
She spoke very briefly of pain.

'You might find yourself Sir, in a manacle,
And you would have to phone us real quick.
That couldn't be classed as a jolly call,
To disentangle's a clever old trick.

It would then, be quite problematical.
To the hospital, we would have to send,
As the problem would be purely medical,
The seat being attached to your end.

I'm sorry I'm being political,
It's the job that makes it so.
My upbringing was strictly clerical,
The daughter of a vicar, you know.'

'Now Sarah, you know I'm amicable,
Making tea whenever you call,
But your shyness is quite pathetical,
Please tell me that word, after all.'

'Hush Sir, you're being too naughty-cal.
I'm going quite red in the face.
I will have to make this a shorty-call,
And rush from this embarrassing place.'

'Oh Sarah, I know you're being tactical,
And believe me, I'm not a prude,
But do you think, it's quite practical,
With all this to avoid being rude?'

Len Hynds

China Dream

My warrior he sings to me
Sings to me in my sleep
Holding me tightly, never letting go
We dance and he holds me
Gliding me cross the floor
As if it were made of glass
My warrior he speaks to me
Tells me of love and life
Wanting to hold me for evermore
I wake and there's no sound
My warrior is gone
Back to a land and time forgotten
I look at the rose in my bedside vase
A petal is falling
Just like the night before.

Jane Cooter

Travels With An Old Sea Dog

The boys thought a boat on the Thames would be fun.
'It sounds different,' I said, with foreboding,
But wrote off for pamphlets and all the know-how,
If only to stop them from goading.

It didn't! They thought it a super idea,
And I must admit I felt excited
At the thoughts of just aimlessly drifting all week
With the dog, and a friend we'd invited.

We loaded the car - enough food for a month!
And arrived at four hours and a quarter.
As I handed our things to my son on the boat
Hark! An ominous 'plop' in the water!

The keys! The car keys were now down ten feet deep.
That's a great start I thought, without hope.
But believe it or not, a young man came along
And retrieved it with magnet and rope.

The boys were both given a lesson of sorts,
Then we left to glide slowly up river.
So quiet and peaceful, with gardens each side,
Then a lock loomed ahead - raised a quiver.

But we followed instructions and sailed through with ease,
And decided to look for a mooring.
A space between boats by a pub and a bridge
Was where we tied up until morning.

We heard a strange noise as we sat in the boat,
Sort of scraping, and somebody hissing.
We didn't dare look, as it gave us a fright,
But next morning a fender was missing.

Well, not to be fazed we continued our way,
But our four-legged friend had decided
No way would she budge to go walkies with us
Until a gangplank was provided.

We threatened to leave her, enticed her with food.
We pulled her - did all we were able.
And then an idea - from inside the boat
And turned upside down - the table!

Now over she strolled with her tail in the air,
And a look of sheer triumph about her.
We went through this ritual three times a day
So that off and on-board she could saunter.

We were soon to reach Oxford, the city of spires,
Where we wandered and did some sightseeing.
Then back to the boat to sail merrily home,
'Goodbye Moley and Toad for the time being.'

We waved to the stork on her nest in the tree,
'Au revoir' to the kingfishers blue.
Our river adventure had come to a close,
But we'd do it again, we all knew.

Brenda D Wymer

My Little Sister

My little sister is great!
She is my best mate
She never lets me down!
She's always around
Rolling about on the ground
My little sister is funny
She's always playing with our bunny!
Who runs around with a dummy
And being like my sis
My little sister is great!
She will always be my best mate.

Courtney Hughes

Summer Daze

Winter sneaks out with a whimper,
Spring ends with a hint of the sun.
Summer starts with a wink and a simper,
And a hint of hot days yet to come.
We hear each day's forecast with gladness,
Look forward to good days henceforth.
Away with all sorrow and sadness,
We're glad we don't live in the north.
Summer is here, sweet, sweet summer,
With barbies al fresco, and all that,
And an incompetent young guitar strummer
Joined in song by the neighbour's tom cat.
Dad, stripped to the waist in his garden
Thinks he's Tarzan, so agile and free,
But we think, just begging his pardon,
He's more like an old chimpanzee.
Mum, mistakenly sheds all her clothing,
No modesty, pride or constraint,
Dad views her with awe touched with loathing
Cos the Venus de Milo she ain't!
Summer, sweet summer is soon over,
Global warming the prophets foretell,
The nudists all think, they're in clover,
Whilst, to others, it's a foretaste of Hell!

Jack Scrafton

The Old Barn

A tumbled-down barn stood at the top of the field
Forgotten, neglected, forlorn,
No longer the animals came to and fro
No longer the men came each morn,
The old barn remembered when there was bustle and noise
Horses and cattle around,
Piles of sweet-smelling hay in the troughs,
The sound when the turnips were ground.
Now seldom anyone came thro' its creaking old doors
No one clambered up into its loft,
Only swallows and martins brought cheer
Oh and mice coming in from the frost.
Hedgehogs came in to spend winter
Safely rolled up in the warm,
A lovely white owl perched high in the rafters
Away from cold winds and the storm.
For the old barn, time passed so slowly
Winters were lonely and long,
Sometimes a tramp, lonely like him
Stayed for the night and was gone.
Then one year when the swallows returned
They found the barn bustling and busy once more,
The doors hung on shiny new hinges,
Its floor thick with clean rustling straw,
Troughs once more full of sweet-smelling hay
The roof no longer leaked rain,
Each day had a new sense of purpose
It was happy and useful again.
Now the barn doesn't stand at the top of the field
Forgotten, neglected, forlorn,
All day the animals come to and fro
The men come again every morn.

Margery Cambridge

Unwanted

Don't tell me how to feel,
You can't see inside
I can't show you
For fear of letting go.
You will never know
Just how much you hurt me
When you didn't
Tell me about her,
Though I knew, deep inside
That you didn't love me anymore,
Hope lived on in each smile,
Each word you said.
Now I know, I was right all along -
I am unwanted,
Once again.

You'll never see me cry these tears,
Or fall apart,
This broken heart,
So many times before by people like you,
You raise me up
And each time I'm dropped further
You tell me I shouldn't feel alone,
I know your type, then you go, too.
Now I know, I was right all along -
I am unwanted,
Once again.

You can't see inside of me,
See this pain that tears me up,
Any more and I'll be no more.
I can't show you how I feel
For fear of letting go.
Though I know deep inside,
Each smile
Each word

Tears me up anew.
This heart, broken in two
Many pieces by people like you.
Now I know, I was right all along -
I am unwanted,
Once again.

Jocelyn Benham

Growing Old

Life's many tragedies that unfold
When people you love grow old
But love should never go cold
To have and enjoy good health
Is to hold onto great wealth
The feet gently warmed at the hearth
Memories of life and love can fade away
To return on another fine day
The family photographs grow dust in the shade
Smiles set on a happy parade
Teeth, flesh and bones that are nature made
My closeness to my parents
Will never turn transparent
While I still exist on this planet
A belief in a strong home
From which to roam
Sometimes to return alone
A hope sometimes exists
Within life's many twists
For fondness and love to persist.

Tim Sharman

Sunflower

Favoured flower of high esteem
Standing tall you reign supreme
Beautiful flower named after the sun
You are the most majestic one
From the lovely rose fair homage is paid
The daisy and marigold bask in your shade
We didn't foresee your size and girth
When we covered your seed with soft spring earth
And now you stand by the garden wall
Glorious, golden and monarch of all.

Jessie Kybird

Jesus Christ

On a journey hard and long
Three wise men had struggled along
They had trudged on through the night
With a star providing the light
A hotel clerk said all spaces were full
But we do know now that that was a 'load of bull'
As in the light from that shining star
There was seen by them a door ajar
For at the back a stable stood
Made of oak - a formidable wood
In utter relief they all did sigh
Then suddenly was heard a Baby cry
A pair in there in parenthood
Known at Joseph and Mary stood
In a manger for its bed
A little Lad did rest His head
The straw was swept as Mary wept
A moment that no Christian can forget
Out of respect the wise men did stir
Passing over gifts of gold, frankincense and myrrh
That star on high - that little Babe's cry
All reasons why - with too our Lord above
Will always try - until we die - to celebrate 'love'.

John Leonard Wright

21 Years

Oh how the years have slipped away,
When I was very young,
I had a son that really made
My day, he is the one,
Now suddenly, though still a mum,
I'm not so needed now,
My lovely son is 21, he really is a wow!
He's made a new life for himself,
With Kim his special friend
One thing for sure I love him more,
I know my love won't end.

He's very kind my young son, Jon,
He visits every week,
And does so many things for me,
You'll always hear me speak,
Of this and that he's done to keep me comfy in my home,
Monday night's my favourite,
That's when my Jon comes home,
While I am not so busy I sit
Down every day,
Writing poetry, hoping I'll manage
To one day,
Write something good enough to please the Forward Press,
I guess if I keep trying I might be a success.
Well anyway I'll try again today,
To send my poem,
21 today I say, I hope perhaps I'll win.

Congratulations Forward Press,
A long time to be sure,
I hope you'll be here publishing
For many, many more.

Eileen Southey

Prayer Of The Children Of Martha

O Lord shew thy mercy upon us

And we will vacuum the carpets
In your cathedrals:
Forgive us the noise of modern invention
That smothers our small supplications.

In village churches,
Where the rush is less urgent,
We will employ a brush
And some mild detergent.

We will scour the stonework and dust the crevices:
Forgive us our scaffolding.
We will burn candles, as of old,
Though electric light has long been installed.

We will put polish on the pews,
Likewise upon the silver and brass:
In winter we will replenish the boiler
For thy frozen people.

We will arrange flowers and arrange services
With pastoral dignity:
And in clean raiment we will
Listen to the Comfortable Words.

We will not suffer our unbiblical dogs
To enter your dwelling place:
Neither will we smoke
In your matchless holy church.

We will embroider hassocks
From the backs of sheep
For other sheep to kneel upon:
The Lord is our shepherd.

We shall supply clean surplices
And take care of the altar linen:
Forgive us our laundry marks
As we forgive them their high prices.

We will exercise our vocal chords
In praise of thy Holy Name:
And listen to the great organ
With the organs of our listening.

We shall show indulgence
To those who regard your house as a museum
And, if the hour is right,
Invite them to join in our Benedicite and Te Deum.

We will put silver in the plate
Or copper in the bag,
As may be more expedient:
Lord forgive us our shortage of change.

With dedication we will perform our duties
And try to keep your Commandments:
Lead us not into the temptations
That beset us and our beloved.

Take not thy Holy Spirit from us.

Mary Nugent

A Soldier

A baby is born, mid anguish and joy
The long wait is over, all pain forgotten
Now God is thanked for the gift of a boy
He'll grow, he'll be upright, a leader of men.

As years pass by at school and beyond
His talents are many, learning is fun
Friendship and fortitude, this is his bond
No more could anyone ask of a son.

But fighting is fierce in a far-off land
To win a just cause, so some would think
And off to a war, there are guns to be manned
He goes, with the blessing of family links.

Son never returns, not alive, that is
Like many before him, bombs won the day
This time, for his mother the pain does *not* pass
Such is the price our families pay.

Evelyn D Alvis

Untitled

I stand here peeling onions
For my first barbecue -
You'd think it strange at sixty-four
Never have I done this before!

I've baked and roasted, fried and grilled,
Umpteen cakes and pasties filled.
My family's grown, I'm now alone,
Eat more simply, lost a stone.

Now young friends with thoughts well meant
Suggested that I use my tent
To have them visit, eat outside,
Do modern stuff on charcoal wide.

That's why I'm scared but happy too,
Trying something totally new.
I've bought the buns and drinks and fish,
Burgers, crisps and choccy dish.

Lights from loft are strung around,
Guitars will bring a joyful sound.
So God bless all these young folk bright,
We'll have a ball tomorrow night!

Sylvia Tolcher

Safe Haven

The pheasant stood amidst the busy road
So much in danger as the cars rushed by,
But when he spread his wings and upward sped
He then was safe amid the deep blue sky.

Our dangers come while anchored to the ground
Confining thoughts to everything around,
But when we lift our hearts to God above
We then are safe, encompassed by His love.

William J Bartram

Forward And Upwards!

Grasp the bottle, with secure grip,
rest it, against waist and hip.
Run thumbnail round, to split the foil,
untwist the wire, from its little coil.

Remove the wire cage, with its seal,
change your grip, so both thumbs can feel
the base of the cork, securing the flow,
gently push upwards 'til it starts to go.

Point away from faces, and wait for the *bang!*
Drink explodes from the bottle, for the assembled gang.
Bubbles frothing, for this celebratory cause,
poured into glasses, amid rapturous applause.

Katie Coles steps forward, to take the stage,
as a Director, Forward Press has come of age.
Twenty-one years, of publishing rhymes,
a tremendous achievement, in these challenging times.

Poets, like me, given a fighting chance
to see their work printed, at a glance,
in professionally bound books, to grace any shelf,
to say with pride, 'I wrote *that* poem, myself!'

When a hobby, or pastime, lays dormant at home,
with nowhere to show it . . . no published tome,
a progressive approach, like Forward Press,
is a welcome respite, I must confess.

Competitive themes, fighting for printed space,
to show other writers, in the winning chase;
a prize at the end? - It's not always needed,
just the satisfaction of knowing, that you've succeeded.

Jim Bell

For Stanley

The poppies are dying
Young men are dead,
Free from their pain.

My heart is heavy
I must go on,
The rain is cold,
Daylight is fading,
Panic and fear are
All around, bodies
Lifeless lay on the ground.

Such a dreadful waste of lives,
Lonely parents, children, wives.
Lost limbs, sight and minds,
War so cruel so unkind,
Missing those we left behind.

Trenches deep of mud, rats and lice,
Clouds of shrapnel blinds the eye,
Again lads in their hundreds die.

Back home the harvest will be
Gathered in, I long to be back there
Again, out of this smoke and
Deafening noise, never-ending
Mud and rain, will I ever see
My home again?

Vivian Chrispin

A Tour Of Essex

Winding roads, country lanes,
Stansted Airport and its planes,
Colchester, the oldest town,
Where Romans marched up and down.

Cressing Temple Barns are old,
Sometimes there, crafts are sold,
Chelmsford is the place to go,
Where shoppers bustle to and fro.

Walton on the Naze, Clacton too,
Sandy beaches with heaps to do,
At Colchester there's lots to see,
Including monkeys in a tree.

In Witham, Dorothy L. Sayers did live,
Her novels had a lot to give,
Her statue is displayed with pride,
Which tourists visit from far and wide.

Wednesdays for Braintree is market day,
Bargains shown in full array,
Many places where it's quaint to eat,
So visit Essex, for a treat.

Susan May Downs

Progress - ABE

Where once there was space and hope
Now to be replaced,
A wonderful winter land of trees and bees
Wildlife flourished and golden memories grew,
Lost forever
By another jungle of despair
A step in time to look back and hope
Where will it all end
The simple things we once knew.

R Sunshine

What We Find

We should all try to get ready for the change in the weather,
We can do it if we try together.

We have to try to make an advance
In today's technology, to monitor and predict seems the only chance.

With the help of radar and satellite we must confine,
Without the proper science and equipment,
What would we do with no trace or sign?

It's up to you too and we have to prepare,
Heavy rainfalls and hurricanes, we need to know where!

We have to do this for all mankind,
It's the best way that's what we find.

John Walker

Untitled

One day, Mother Earth, I shall cease to walk upon your hallowed turf.
I shall be silenced at a time and place indefinable by me;
But ironically, in ceasing to live I shall become part of you,
For my body, tho' dust and ashes, will return to your eternal crust
                                  from whence I first came,
To thus exist as a human fossil in perpetuity.
My spirit also will forever live, of that I am certain,
For my spirit is me, my inner being, my soul,
And that cannot be destroyed by fire or decomposition.
Therefore I am really indestructible and though in death invisible,
Yet will I live, as my ubiquitous spirit floats through your
                                  spacious firmament,
Freely roaming, but indubitably yours, Mother Earth.

Malcolm F Andrews

Cat In A Window

Black and white cat
resident between
sagged red curtains
and streaked glass.
Whiskers twitching.

I wonder
if he knows I watch him
while he observes the passing scene.

Languid licking of paw,
metronome flick betrays his undisciplined tail
until,
stretching elastically
he curls
nose buried into fur.

Our world never penetrates his business
as the business is his own.

Alison Bainbridge

The Promise

I sit alone, a mind clouded with daydreams
wondering why you have not come into my life,
picturing the contours of your face
and wishing you were more than just a vision.
I feel you near, almost touched by the warmth of your body
the gentle aroma of yesterday's scent
and then you are gone.
I imagine the day when I finally find you
the joy, the excitement of that destined time,
the promise fulfilled to find my eternal love
walking towards you with arms open.
Listen, can you not hear me call your unspoken name
messages carried on the breeze
to caress your unseen face,
I have so much to tell you, show you, give you
I wait patiently for that fated day
our eyes meet and I will know
that you are more than just a vision . . .

Julie Zacharia

Untitled

A Friday in August
And the wheeze of the 5 o'clock train
Disgorging the usual collection
Of rumpled suits at the station:
Haggard middle managers
And assistant chief executives, bleary
From the strain of wearing that bright smile.
At some point along that homeward stretch of rail
The faces all collapsed in lines of worry.

Arriving at this moment, this instant,
This section of eternity:
The radiant air a glow of expectation
These high clouds streaming wisps
Against the far, far blue
These birds that dart and sweep among the heavens
And in the west a blaze of white hot gold.
Not evening yet and time remains
And shall they? Shall they stop and turn again?

Ian Barth

Autumn

Autumn leaves come tumbling down
Yellow, red and golden brown
Little creatures scurrying around
Seeking hedgerows, trees and ground
Squirrels, hedgehogs, field mice too
All know what they have to do
Build little nests firm and stout
To keep the cold of winter out
They find all the food that's best
To store away for winter's rest
Then snug and warm they'll settle in
Before the winter storms begin
Now snow and ice can blow around
But they are all safe and sound
Till one day they sniff the air
A warmer sweeter scent is there
Why goodness me, it's time to wake
To yawn, to stretch, to give a shake
Spring again is at the door
The trees are turning green once more.

Dorie Buckman

Compass For Life!

Fair weather faith does not enhance,
We need the wind to blow
To learn to trust Almighty God,
His strength and power to know!
For when we sail on tranquil seas
All calm and trouble free,
We cannot learn to put our trust
In God's ability!
We need the battering of the waves
Against our small frail barque
To understand His purposes,
Be guided through the dark
Of times when rescue seems afar,
And waves above us tower.
Yet when our boat is sinking
This the time to prove His power!
Faith grows through tribulation
When exercised with ease,
And prayer becomes our compass
To guide through stormy seas!

Elizabeth Bruce

Sweet Mother

(For my mum who died 6 months ago)

Each and every day I think of you, since you went away
I have felt so sad and blue.
My mother I miss you so much now you are not here,
you were so wonderful, kind and dear.
My friend your sweetness and sense of humour was fun,
I have been so lonely, you were like the summer sun.
You were thoughtful and always wanted a cuddle,
sometimes you did not mind being in a muddle.
It is getting a little better but they say time does heal.
One thing for sure you always loved a good meal.
Always you said there was no one like your mother,
that is so true, there is never another.
I have such good friends who are helping me through,
the sadness I feel inside since the day I lost you.
A husband who loves me and a dog called Ben,
we had some laughs when we talked about men.

Sally Warren

Goodbye My Love

(Dedicated to my husband Brian who died 28.03.09)

Death is so final, your life has now gone
Your memories however will still linger on
To sit there beside you, your life ebbing away
Was torture for me with every new day

First were the strokes then the cancer came
You bore it all, especially the pain
You inspired the patients that shared your ward
With your courage and humour, they were not bored

So many memories - some good and some bad
The bad disappear - the good make me sad
I look to the future, you are still all around
Up in your study and here on the ground

I hope you are happy now and suffering no more
You did not deserve the pain that you bore
I was not ready for you to go
But your life had been taken so long ago.

Sylvia Coverdale

Resurrection

Summer is dead;
Who took her life?
Autumn embraced her in his cruel grip;
Tore off her gaudy garments one by one
And left her poor bones bare
Sketched dark against the morning's pallid sky.
The rising sun took pity on her state
And tried in vain to warm her outstretched limbs;
Yet still some life remains
Deep within those fragile seeming twigs
And will emerge again in new green growth;
Blossom in many a tender hue and sweet perfume
Will come once more to welcome tardy Spring
When Winter's reign comes to his bitter end,
And singing birds will find a nesting place, amongst dense foliage.
Thus has it ever been,
Thus will it always be
Until the crack of doom.

Phyllis Bush

A Plea For A Poet

(In which the reader is begged to pray
to a lady who's most wondrous fair
to show our poet the noble way
to drive our enemies to despair):

As our poet strikes a heroic pose
fit for fighting mortal foes
his pen sharp'd to a steel-tipped point
his printer primed with every font
his shield traced with raised fists
his name entered in all the lists
his courser decked with banners gay
ready at all hours for the fray;
Offer a prayer to the gentle muse
that she'll with inspiration him infuse
and with venomous spleen his barbs inspire
to burn the 'powers that be' with fire;
And grant he may perceive the truth
for which few today can find a proof
and fewer still do care to see;
'Tis sure a strange philosophy
that on such rare commodity
so little value placed be.

Simon Muscatt

Roses In Summer

Rambling roses stray across the stone wall,
pushing their golden heads against each other
each one endeavouring to be the centre of attention;
assured of its own perfection
- survival is to be noticed -
for who knows of their existence if no one catches sight of them?

Travellers passing by are not disappointed
as they slow down on the narrow road,
attention caught, momentarily,
with fleeting admiration for the vivid yellows and greens,
bustling against the ochre-coloured stone.

She opens the creaky wooden door: their nemesis,
red straw hat perched on greying locks,
bright gaudy flowers fighting for space over her ample frame.
Brandishing secateurs in her wrinkled hands,
and taking her own life in hand,
she edges carefully along the narrow pavement towards them.
Her aim: to cut their vanity down to size.

Unsure of whose time has come,
they push forward even harder
to prove that they are the fittest, the brightest.
Does she not realise that without them the bush would fade and wither?
Do they not realise that they will each waste away,
their unique importance dissipating, when new life sprouts?

She inspects her prize blooms with an air of serenity:
it has taken years to provide such a show of strong, proud,
dignified, golden roses.
Lovingly she touches their delicate petals,
recalling her own babies' soft young skin.
Eyes closed, she cups a bloom in her hand,
bowing her head to breathe in its delicate perfume,
distant summer days flood her mind.

New passers-by witness this tenderness as a moment in time
but for her it stays much longer.
Memories of these proud flowers
will remain with her throughout the stark winter months.

Gently, without malice, she snips the fading flowers into her basket,
all they feel is their importance drawing to an end
- and the unfairness of it -
all she is doing is giving other delicate blooms a chance to shine through
- prolonging the summer and life.

Kate Higgins

Twenty-One Years

(For Chloë and Charlotte, my two wonderful daughters)

Twenty-one years of knowing you so well,
raising you as best I could, hoping you'd turn out alright!
And you did of course, for how else could it be?
The nurturing of Mother Love, nature's true hand deep in the soil of my heart.
Nowhere else was there space big enough for you to grow.
Nowhere else was there a love so deep to nourish my soul . . .
and give me twenty-one years of knowing you so well.
Dependent no more, a woman of the world,
my heart embraces that which is you.
From the realms of the ocean to the height of the stars,
from the air that I breathe - to the depths of my soul;
I have twenty-one years of knowing you so well!

Amanda Robbins

Churchill - The Valiant Man

He was born wrapped in the Union flag crying, 'Empire'
A proclamation of which he would never tire
Born to serve King and country
Land of hope and glory, mother of the free

First Lord of the Admiralty and his beloved fleet
Rule Britannia, the country no one will never beat
'Winston's back' the famous signal, he's at the helm
The staunchest defender of the realm

'We will never surrender', his example great
Defeating our enemies his destiny and fate
His inborn traits, courage, resolution and defiance
He rallied the countries of the Union and Empire into an alliance

In the face of Hitler's threat he would not cower
The eighth of May 1945 his finest hour
Valiant and true, his patriotism an example to all
'The Empire and freedom,' his rallying call.

Colin N Crews

Magic Oft Told

The magic oft told . . . by the bards of old
of autumn trees bold . . . in cloak of gold

Winter trees now bare . . . still impressive there
and without a care . . . for spring will repair

So thank God again . . . for that winter's rain
for where leaves have lain . . . His snowdrops will reign

Then a sweet new green . . . again will be seen
song birds will preen . . . in the summer scene

Valerie Ovais

One Year After Bernni
(RIP 3-9-08)

Her mother sat and stared,
A 1,000 memories . . . as I entered,
House and farm looked the same,
As tho' I'd never left a childhood game . . .
Memories relived through our tears,
Questions! Shock! Loss and fears!
Why did her daughter, one year ago, die?
Why cancer - no treatment - how and why?
I suggested, supported, and with a cry,
Respecting dignity and empathy
Recognising her need was not for sympathy
But a quest to find and understand
This harsh card she cannot comprehend . . .
To lose a child aged fifty,
Who went to school with me,
The cruellest blow to a mother,
For this cannot equal another . . .
In her kitchen we sat a while,
Feeling pain through tear and smile,
Unable to ease her terrible aching,
I hugged her before finally parting . . .

Liz Edmonds

Maybe

Forward Press, twenty-one today
Unlocking dreams to see a poem in print
Some happy, others sad
Memories of times gone by
Tragedies we will never forget
Floods, storms, wars
These things happen over twenty-one years
The world changes, we grow older
But the flowers still bloom
Lambs play in the fields
Trees grow and lose their leaves
The rivers flow their endless way
Sun shines and snow arrives
I wish I had a crystal ball
To look at the next twenty-one years
Forward Press still going strong
Poems for all to read
Peace in the world
Maybe.

Doris Warren

Book Of Life

We met when the pages on the Book of Life were new,
Not much to tell then - experiences few.
With the trials and tribulations of this new age -
We learned from the world when we entered its maze.
Of life with its crossroads and many dead ends,
Frustrations and tears, its meandering bends.
We could not know what the future foretold,
And we struggle blindly onwards to keep a firm hold.
And the pages of the book, slowly they fill,
As we journey through life, down valleys - up hills.
Our experiences are written, for always, for keeps,
Nothing is omitted - the Writer never sleeps.
And in the year when I met you,
Our pathways entwined, we'd found friendship renewed.
It's easier now, that road we must tread,
All the obstacles seem smaller - there's nothing to dread,
For true friendship helps us be strong,
Giving us the courage to carry on.
So thanks for the friendship, loyalty and trust,
While the Writer writes on 'til we turn into dust.

Debbie Curtis

Picture Of Enchantment

(The Old Mill 'at peace')

Hills, flowing silently down to the water's edge
Wild flowers, spread across the meadow's floor
So delicate in colour and form
Trees gather themselves in bouquets, painting
Valley and lea in a disorganised array.

An old mill house stands alone and idle
As if waiting for the past to catch up with the future
Its heart no longer pulsating, just dallying until
A new dawn arrives.

Sea birds cackle and squawk as they skim
The dappled surface of the old mill pond
Marsh land, hopes for the turn of the tide. So as
To immerse itself in life once more

Boats run aground, held by chains wrapped round bollards.
Meditating, will they sail again?
Yachts, bob and curtsy as the tide comes and goes
Rhythmic in its restless energy.

'Bem' the badger, slowly makes his way across
The old mill bridge lost in thought of a new day
Dusk advances slowly pushing day's brightness
Aside, letting all rest in peace

Where am I you ask,
'I am in Heaven,' is my reply.

E A Turner

The Last Garden

I'm going to the last garden, to keep my mind clear,
With peace in my heart,
To a place where the robin perches on a branch,
Singing his song.
I gaze in amazement at the wonder of nature,
Then I realised it was all worthwhile,
And you're not that far away from me,
Because you never went away.
Your spirit is close by my side in the last garden,
To keep my mind clear of trivia and the mundane,
To show me a new life with nature.
You gave me strength to carry on.
I'm going to the last garden,
Where squirrels bounce animatedly along,
Searching for their nuts.
I'm going to the last garden,
Where the gulls fly low above my head,
Swirling and soaring through their own flight of freedom,
Gliding in the damp air.
I will return again to the last garden,
To see all the things that so many people have forgotten,
What so many people miss in their materialistic lives.
I'm going to the last garden to keep my mind clear,
With peace in my heart.

Lou Crouch *(RIP 26.1.09)*

River Of Babylon
(With apologies to Lord Tennyson)

On either side the river lie
Long fields of barley and of rye.
And leisurely it makes its way,
Starting its journey at the break of day.
No need to hurry as it glides gently by.
Reflecting on its surface a cloudless sky.
Before noon it will be floating through a town,
Which boasts a cathedral of some renown.
Its stained glass windows now heavy with grime,
Can still let in the sunlight, most of the time.
Tall buildings stand proud on the riverbank.
Office blocks, tower blocks, rank upon rank.
The river has changed colour now to muddy-brown,
As it picks up the detritus of this ancient town.
Within its depths, though not so deep
Swim hungry fish who a vigil keep,
Darting to and fro they watch night and day
To see what the townsfolk might throw away.
A lump of bread? Who can tell,
Some juicy maggots would go down well!
But alas, the days of anglers are no more,
Sparkling clean waters here are now folklore.
The filth of the turgid river's flow
Hinders the freedom of where it has to go.
Past the flour mill and through the town,
Under a road bridge near the Rose & Crown.
Here it picks up a crisp packet or two,
Then a plastic tube that once held glue.
Now last week's news of the football scores
And screaming headlines of Afghan wars.
All ignored by the passers-by
Who add to the junk with a half-eaten pie.
Carelessly dumped still inside its foil tray,
To slowly poison the river, day by day.
Just a few yards on, resting near the verge,
Is a supermarket trolley, half submerged.
And wedged against a slimy green stone
Lies a red and white road menders cone.
Pram wheels and bikes lie rusting on its bed

While dead kittens in a bin bag float overhead.
Now it's passing the shopping mall
And its nearby concrete car park sprawl.
Here vehicles are lined up like orderly troops,
Awaiting loads of chicken, frozen chips and soups,
Discarded wrappers and empty boxes,
Left there to attract rats and urban foxes.
Now the waters hurry to be near
The frothy, bubbling, tumbling weir
Which will oxygenate and cleanse its soul,
To help it flow freely now towards its goal.
And as it progresses further still,
It passes the derelict sawyers mill.
Nobody there now to arrest its flow,
It has a more important place to go.
Onward now through the rest of the day,
Serene and peaceful as it glides on its way.
Ignoring villages and woods on either side,
It can now slow its pace to an easy ride.
And as the sun sinks now so low,
With only a few more miles to go,
Does the river have memories of this day's dawn
And the tranquillity of life where it was born?
Or of open country where horizon meets sky,
Where the corn stands tall and skylarks fly
And on either side the river lie,
Long fields of barley and of rye?
No point now when it's where it was meant to be,
Meeting up with the tide of the great North Sea.

Margaret M Bell

The New Year

Well here we are, into another new year,
It's the first of January and winter is here,
The gardens are covered under a carpet of white
All thanks to Jack Frost who arrived in the night,
With ice-cold fingers he's painted windows and doors
Many beautiful patterns, of ferns and more,
Long icicles hanging from gutters and pipes
That shine like silver in the cold morning light,
Branches bowed down under drifts of snow
Where a blackbird sits huddled, reluctant to go,
For everywhere is quiet, all is muffled and still,
A moment of peace, of joy, and goodwill.

Jean Harding

A Bitter Tomorrow

If I was to die tomorrow
Would anybody miss me?
If I was to die in sorrow
Would anybody kiss me?
Just to say goodbye
As they stand with
Their head hung low
Screaming out why.

Or would life just carry on
As though I'd never been,
Never been heard,
Thought of or seen?
Would anybody struggle
To cope with me not there
If I was to die tomorrow
Would anybody care?

Marvyn B Candler

Reflections

I once was an 8, I'm now an 18
So please don't be shocked by my weight gain extreme
I had a flat tummy but now it is round
My former self
Has surely drowned.

Dragged into waters so deep in despair
I fear I will not find a way out of there
My healthy body
So vital and sound
Is submerged underwater
And yet to be found.
I have been unwell for such a long time
Which is why myself left me
With this new body of mine.

The good can be seen in the form of my child
Yet, still I dream that the waters so wild
Uncover my real body
And wash it ashore
So I can reclaim it
And wear it once more.

Denise Dowdell-Stent

The Gypsy Firedance

Around an immense roaring fire they fly,
Against the backdrop of a sunset sky,
Squashing the grass with their shiny black boots,
Singing the songs of their Romany roots.
With pearly white teeth and curly black hair,
And dark black eyes with a hard steely stare,
They dance and dance by the light of the fire,
As the tall flames reach higher and higher.
The girls in long skirts, with hoops in their ears,
And white frilly blouses, dance amid claps and cheers.
The men stamp out the beat, and kick up the dirt,
Each wearing black trousers and a white ruffled shirt.
Faster and faster the violinists play,
Whilst seated in a row on a large bale of hay.
The night air is filled with their music for hours,
Along with the perfume of night jasmine flowers.
The fire glows orange and red on their skin,
Its light drawing hundreds of fireflies in,
Illuminating their ornate caravan parked nearby,
Whilst they dance on and on 'neath the starry night sky.

Julie Wealleans

Untitled

My place of work was once a happy place
But now I find it very hard to face
There's an air of gloom when one walks through the factory gate
Wondering what will be our fate
Order books are now very low
Losing our jobs would be quite a blow
Gone is the banter we once enjoyed
As we face up to being unemployed
Some think we will survive
But not if we're given our P45!

B Dennis

The Secret Alcoholic Drinker

I'm the secret alcoholic drinker
I'm a very deep thinker
You'd never now how much I've had
I guess it's really rather sad,
From such a promising lad.

The buzz I get
I never forget
To feel so ease
No trouble to please
And all my worries roll into one,
Until they become none.
I can touch my dream
Not afraid or fleeing.
The confidence I have
Keeps me from being sad,
Such a promising lad.

Where did it all go wrong?
Why couldn't I be more strong?

I know I must be in control
Of my dear old friend, *alcohol.*

Glen Noakes

Life

I packed my bag, I cannot stay,
I'm a teenage boy who ran away.
To live on the streets that's all I know,
No job, no money, nowhere to go.
Wearing tatty blue jeans and a white hoodie top,
Trainers which came from a charity shop.
I beg from strangers who bypass me,
I may be lucky and get 50p.
Seeing alcoholics with their bottles drinking cider or beer,
Drug addicts using needles all through the year.
Life on the streets is so hard to bear,
With no one to love you or show that they care.
Now darkness has fallen, it's time to find shelter to sleep,
Living among the down and outs where our homes are the street.

Jennifer Withers

Tenderly

Fall now tenderly to the ground,
need to be lost
before you can be found
try not to ache a heart
you won't always be around.

Things never seem as great as they sound.

Ria Blackwell

Valley Pond

The way down by steep path,
Well worn clay track trod through the grass.
Careful one don't fall,
Don't want a call,
To help one out the brambles,
Onwards scramble
A mud puddle,
Blocking the pathway.
Detour way, way
Of tall hawthorns
Careful of their thorns, they cut like wire.

On the valley floor
Nature open her beauty drawer,
To a beautiful forest pond,
With bags of yellow iris flags wands
The pond carpeted one end,
By green lily pads
On which yellow wagtails, time spend,
Rapid water ripples
Made by small fish.
Diving flash of blue
A kingfisher fishing.

Bryan Clarke

They Took Our Vicar Away

Last Sunday they took our vicar away,
They say it's only for a short stay.
Poor chap it's in his head, they said.
He said we were to rise from the dead!
Standing in the pulpit between hymns
He started going on about God's whims,
About God not wanting to hear the groans
From poor old Mrs Jones with broken bones,
We could do her weekly shopping
To save her so much hopping.
He said God appreciated our endless talk
But could we take the young cripple for a walk
Perhaps to the park or around town.
My dear, how could I, I'd never live it down!
Then he went on about God's test
To take us out in our Sunday best
To a place where weeds abound
And for us to prostrate on the ground
Because the vicar was finding it hard
To maintain his beloved churchyard.
God said we could also tend His flock
Visit the housebound in the tower block
Cut our flowers when visiting the ill,
After all it is God's will
And we surely shall be blessed
Besides your vicar needs a rest.
I hardly need to say we were astounded
At this practical Christianity he expounded
And I could see a few who left their pew
Muttering about vicars and churches anew.
Well, I was wide awake and decided to stay
But really I prefer to doze the sermon away.
And I wonder, my dear, if God did stay
Last Sunday, when they took our vicar away.

Vic Sutton

Newborn

We never think of the consequences,
We never think of the risks,
When we are born we are immune,
Of the dangers that exist.
We never think of the danger,
We never think of the past,
When we are born we are unaware
Of the life that may not last.
We never think of the reasons,
We never think of the risks,
When we are born we are immune
Of the dangers that exist.

As a newborn to the world
We only know the love you show
Of our surroundings, parents love
Of our only family.
So as we grow and learn to live
We need to know the ways,
Someone has to guide us, show us,
Educate and protect us,
It's a tough world in which to grow
For a newborn.

Christine Rands

The Man On The Roof

I look through my window
He catches my eye
The man on the roof
Stands tall against the sky
He's always there
Whether the weather
Is stormy or fair

I feel attracted to him
I wonder why
Because he's only a figment
Of my imagination
In reality it's a tree
But when it catches my eye
It's a great comfort to me

You see I'm disabled
And pleasures are few
Truth is man on the roof
I'm in love with you.

J Pruden

The Great War

This was to be the carnage of the century,
A chapter in life that should have never been,
Destruction of mankind as never seen before,
A hopeless, bloody, senseless war,
Innocent young men so bravely born,
Would soon be cut down like sheaves of corn,
Field Marshall Haig's plea,
'Your country needs you now,' was a far-off cry,
With no guarantee whether you live or die,
Men volunteered to do their best,
Some not knowing they would soon be laid to rest,
Soon the fields of Flanders would be covered in red,
Blood of the dying and those already dead,
The battlefields Ypres, Passchendaele and the Somme
Why all this carnage, what has gone wrong?
Questions remaining for those still fighting and hanging on,
For loved ones back home would be left to mourn,
With the awakening of each new day,
So many heartaches, so many tears,
Will remain with them forever along with the passing years,
So let us not forget other wars,
For the sake of future generations, there will be no more.

Don Carpenter

Untitled

Oh, dear prince, you may be king,
And if that day should come,
You could have a prime minister
Who dearly loves a son.
If you could get together
Be brave and bold and true
We could have a land of plenty
And bring back our boys in blue.

Ban computer, planes and cars
We'd all get used to that
Let us learn and manage
Before there is no choice
Bird flu, swine flu,
Britain rules the waves
Or will the waves rule us?

Sue Baker

War

The silence is chilling
Except for the sound
Of a dog howling
And a weeping child
Who doesn't understand
Why her mother is not there
To hold her hand
For the sands run red
In this hot and humid land
What next they fear
For the bloody day before
Left broken hearts and more
For the sands run red
Much deeper than before
As it did today
As it will tomorrow
On this barren land
The rivers will flow
Of the tears that will flood
The land of broken souls.

Patricia Carr

Flagstone Blues

I'm a pedestrian, me
Bottom of the pile
Hoodies *whoosh* on mountain bikes
I just seethe a while

I'm a pedestrian, me
Looking for a chair
Not to train a lion
But all the 'Staffies' there

I'm a pedestrian, me
Crashed into and abused
Left to perish on the path
Among the phlegm and poos

I'm a pedestrian, me
My pavement a cycle track
iPod whizzers hurtle past
To smash me in the back

I'm a pedestrian, me
The thicko dodger elite
I owe my life to leather
And think upon my feet.

Paul Tricker

The Robins

A sweet little robin with a breast of bright red
came into my garden waiting to be fed.
I looked out next morning and what did I see?
Two little robins waiting for me!
They hopped round the garden and looked everywhere,
looking for somewhere they both could share.
They found an old flowerpot hidden away,
then built their nest in it the very next day.
She sat on the nest and her first egg she lay,
until there were five laying one every day.
She kept them all warm all morning and night,
then turned them all over and sat on them tight.
The two little robins did patiently wait,
while the little cock robin looked after his mate.
Soon the eggs hatched and there in the nest,
were five little chicks all taking a rest.
These little chicks were naked and bare,
huddled together in the nest that they share.
But soon they had feathers just like their mum,
all in the nest catching the sun.
But then came the day when it was real sad,
the little chicks flew and left Mum and Dad.

Margaret Lee

A Compliment To Love

Holding her hand throughout the night
as the fog gently passes from sight
her incandescent beauty was that of a woman loved
the climates of her smiles could guide the migrating
birds for the stars above
into the stillness of dawn when I look into her eyes
the sun is just about to set when she kisses me in warming sighs
her breath fills me with hope and elation
a softness within her lips that causes such
a banquet of sensations
we're close even when not near
her the running water and me the drying tear
I follow her into the day but I long for the night
when she is laying in my arms and it is just the two of us
and the street lamps burning bright.

Emma Bacon

Freedom Of Erin

To walk the land and know the joy
Of freedom in your heart and mind
Is happiness and ties unbound
Unfettered leash and laws unsigned.

Jo Sparkes

My Love

I saw her once as she caught my eye
She smiled, and lit up a summer's sky,
My heart jumped and leapt with joy
For a queen had smiled upon a common boy.

How can I say what was in my heart,
From that one enchanting glance?
I must go back to whence I came
To see again my queen of hearts.

And as I returned to the place of my dreams
Would I see again my queen of queens?
She was there in wondrous splendour
And I was once again in deep surrender.

Again she smiled and waved to me
'Come sit with me and talk awhile'
And with thumping heart I sat beside
The girl who, one day, would be my bride.

It came to pass that one day in May
We announced aloud our 'special day'.
From that day on there would always be
A lifetime of happiness for my love and me.

William Clements

Scavengers In The Metropolis

Scavenging must be a robust activity
I used to think until that day when I saw three
bodies, old, bent and crazy, on the main tourist drag.

Like an old ox the man pulled a cage-like container
Full of plastic bags. From the top of a double-decker
I attempted to calculate the weight of his burden.

Where was he taking it? To the City Council, to get
paid by the load: £5 for half a ton, ten for a ton? Or more?
After all it saves them hiring trash-pickers.

It wasn't long after, I saw another across the road.
An old woman bent over, her white hair
a contrast to the dirty rags that covered her body.

She had just taken dumped plastic bags out of
the rubbish bin by the bus stop, and rolling each
carefully, tight and small, was putting them in one big bag.

Heading for the same place as the man up the road?
A smaller trolley, her load not as big, perhaps being a woman,
she was favoured with positive discrimination.

It was too much to see another scavenger the same afternoon.
Not old and decrepit this time but in mid-life, she had
black plastic bin liners tied across her waist, covering part

of her gypsy skirt, the folds displaying grease and squalor.
The face half covered with a torn scarf, a few ringlets
escaping the tight knot. She was moving her hand

as if it were a bird on a journey to another land.
The smile deepens, the eyes move further away.
The bus arrives, all waiting get on, but not her.

Rani Drew

Rising Tide

Spirit within
surface of skin,
held in that cage,
turning each page,
reading each line,
serving its time,
waits for the rising tide.

Forward, retreat,
keeping its beat,
spirit still sleeps.
Ocean of deeps
pulled by the moon,
midnight to noon,
lifts with the rising tide.

So long the spirit has been
grounded in body's soil.
Now turns the flood of green,
ending the body's toil.
Spirit, unbound,
seeking new ground,
floats on the rising tide.

Heather Enid Wells

Dance

When I was young I loved to dance
All over England and even France
In the street or dance hall
I've been there, done it all
With Brylcream hair
And jazzy suits, I didn't have a care
The girls would queue up to dance with me
If I was hard up, charge a small fee
Now it's no teeth, no Brylcream hair
Life can be so unfair
With my Zimmer in an old folk home
At least I'm not alone
Some of the old dears still like to dance
And often I take a chance
I dance with Flo
We take it slow
Well, she's ninety-three
And can hardly see
Then there's Ann
She gets up when she can
And Maud she holds my hand
Oh isn't love grand
The others just hand jive
Well, it keeps them alive
I think the old men hate me
They dive in when I go for a pee
But there's plenty for all
If only they loosen up we could have a ball
But I know when I die
I'll be dancing in the ballroom in the sky.

Richard Trowbridge

Ice Maiden

Let me linger in the sorrow of your eyes
and I will wander in their loneliness;
through boundless deeps adorned with moonlit skies
where solitude has made its saddest shrine.
There, in the inner sanctum of your lies
I'll read the tender truth you must confess,
though all your soft illusions would disguise.
Then surely you will own that you are mine.

Don't fight it! Nor let scornful words confound
the dreams so gently veiled by your reproach.
For when our hot, enraptured lips are bound
and sealed with burning kisses, love must be.
Your barbs of ice will melt before my touch
and you will yield, and give yourself to me.

Steve Waterfield

Posterity

If I could make one mark on time
With one idea, one single line
Or thoughts collected in one book
Provoking thought in one who'd look
Then one satiated soul I'd be
To have realised one's posterity . . .

Carl Dines

The Hunter And The Hunted

Is that what courtship is all about?
    The hunter and the hunted?
Is that why it is called courtship?
    The hunted being court?
No, surely there is more to love than that?

The hunter plays a pretty game
    Enticing, ensnaring with skill, no shame.
With gentle words and fun-filled days.
    Caresses, promised dreams, a hundred ways
For the hunter to play his game.

The hunted feels no fear or alarm.
    She loves the chase, sees no harm.
Revels in gifts, soft touches and attention.
    Adores the man, seeing no faults to mention
For the hunted to have doubts.

Perhaps it is only when the hunt is over
    The hunted court, no longer free to rover.
That the hunter stops his game, starts to be true.
    Before the truth about the other they had no clue
To know the real people hidden within.

Yes, this is the time when at last true love finds a way
    To accept and love the other come what may.
Differences permitted, speaking your truth - risky and daring
    Forgiving faults, giving space, stopping judging, sharing.
Joined in true love thus allowing space and freedom to be real.

Surly this is what love is all about?

Willing to say their truth, honest about who they want to be.
    Asking for their inner needs, giving sucker to the he and she.
Free to feel, express joy, anger, rage, no emotions can they bar.
    Hearing and seeing each other for who they really are.
No longer hunted or hunter, but liberated, free to be.

Yes, this is what love is all about.
    Knowing that true love will always find a way
To accept and love the other come what may,
    Knowing and being who they are
For true love knows no bar.

Esmé Wilson-Staniforth

Losing A Loved One Is No Easy Thought

When I was but a toddler my first taste of death was my pet rabbit -
But within a few weeks he had been replaced and life went on -
When I reached the ripe old age of ten or eleven -
My lovely dog ceased to meet me at the gate - he had gone -
And my father took me to the stables to see the horses run!
And life went on -
When I turned eighteen and met a boy I married -
My aunt could not attend the wedding - but then she was over eighty -
And when she passed on I regretted her going - but *wow!*
I was soon expecting my first son -
So life goes on!
My thirtieth birthday was very special - not for the reason you would dream -
My father left hospital after a heart attack - alas something else was wrong -
He died as I held my third son's hand - so sad -
Still - life must go on!
Many great aunts flittered throughout my married life -
Until they flittered no more - likewise we felt so strong -
Until my mother died - and then I didn't -
Want life to go on!
My husband used to try to cheer me up - by saying she is only lost -
And we shall find her before too long -
But then the grandchildren appeared and I stopped looking -
Everyone knows that life must go on!
And now I stand here all alone - just memories to keep me young -
And as I stand at window sill - I look beyond -
At all the lives I knew before so even now - I still whisper -
Life must go on!

Valerie Cubitt

Rose Petals And Lavender

Rose petals and lavender
mark where you lay
close by at hand
I can visit each day
there in the shadows
at the edge of life's view
when I hear a whisper
I'll know that it's you
there in the sunshine
the snow and the rain
when I stop to listen
I'll hear you again
so close at hand
yet so far away
for rose petals and lavender
mark where you lay.

Daphne Cornell

Only Love Survives

(For Cai)

Just as you do now, my grandson,
Your father, when young, also learned
How best to defend himself,
By working progressively through very tough
Graded assessments, coloured belts of skill,
Culminating in that final cherished black,
Expressed for you in explosive karate,
And for him in energetic kick-boxing attack.

Sadly, as you know, a few years ago,
On foreign soil, he was suddenly caught
Unawares by and unprotected from weaponry
Used by a ruthless foe,
And tragically, from injuries sustained, he died,
Some say courageously, but for those
Of us who truly loved him,
It was a sacrifice just too far.

And now, dear grandson,
Do be assured that your own
Heredity has not died,
For in interests, profile and ready smile,
You are indeed your father's son,
As he is mine, and within us both
His personal characteristics still live on.

What has also survived are memories,
Treasured recollections of him kept fresh
In our minds through words chosen
To best reflect the loss and undying affection
We feel, and now poignantly inscribed
Upon his Garden of Remembrance headstone,
An affirmation that the love we share
As a family will never die.

Andrew Farmer

Beach Pebble Sculpture

A small stone rests, its iron
is real but diffuse.
In the tumbling of tides
it was shaped and mellowed,
turning to abstract sculpture.

It has the curves, almost, of
thigh or haunch or shoulder blade,
coldness of touch therefore strange,
the lack of creature warmth.

In the exhibition we could
have slipped it into a case
with ironstone pieces from the hands
of Moore, Hepworth, Skeaping,
having it safely taken
for one of those maker's work -
who might even have picked this.

Untitled, begun as land
stolen, then ground down, down,
by other harsher stones -
sea-milled geology -
sleek at last as an otter.

Jane Wight

21 Years Of Fame

Pop the corks and drink a toast
21 years of poetry, you can boast,
Congratulations, you do well to feel proud
As we sing your praises, long and loud,
So many friends, sharing a bond so true
Seeing our words in print, all thanks to you,
Poems are paintings, described in lyrical rhyme
To be loved and appreciated, for all time,
So! Tip your glasses and have a refill
And make sure that bubbly doesn't overspill,
That Forward Press has truly come of age
And worthy of a bow, on the literary stage,
May you keep going for many a long year
Letting us amateur poets, express ourselves clear
Hip hip hooray and may God bless
All the staff and printers of Forward Press.

Barbara Daniels

Untitled

Look at a feather, any feather
The feather of a sparrow or a swan.
Study the line of it and ponder,
Gaze at the beauty of it, look upon
The quill, pliant, keeled to wander
Through space. Fashioned to take on
Every drift and turn asunder
Doubt. Look on the curve on
The plumes modelled for weather
Harsh or soft and marvel on
The colours muted or richer
Then the rarest silk. Put finger on
The down to insulate the tender
Life within. Who designed such wonder?

N Creina Glegg

Temptation

I saw it in the window
As I sauntered past the shop
It seemed to say 'come buy me'
So I felt I had to stop

I really didn't need it
But was tempted just the same
The colour was just perfect
In I went and left my name

They said they would keep it
Just for a day or two
So I could make my mind up
What I really wanted to do

It seemed a little shabby
And it really was quite small
Was I having second thoughts,
Would it really suit me at all?

I thought about it all that day
Then decided that was that
I knew I really had to have it
So I went in and bought the cat.

Irene Kenny

Reunion

Happy, laughing drink.
The kind that makes you think . . .
of all absurdities
drawn of memories,
deeply treasured,
filled with laugher.

Never measured
friends of youth,
of naïve truth
pass the time.
Childhood friends
of never ends.

Old age preys,
always slays.
Look to each other
as sister and brother.
Raise your glasses
or time will pass us.

Sally Plumb

Patience

Learning to wait consumes my life,
Consumes and feeds as well!
Where I have loved, I've loved in strife,
That love I could not tell.
I saw it vanish into hate
Because I hadn't learned to wait!

And this I declare because I know
That were I to love again
I will not tell the seed to grow
Nor grind unripened grain.
But silent in my blissful state
Serve love, having learned to wait.
All that I have grasped at I have lost
All I relinquished, won.
The marriage of two minds
At best deceives, till all is done.
And love, the conqueror
Yields to fate
Stronger, having learned to wait!

Gary Peters

Great Aunt Jane

Great Aunt Jane
Alights from the train
In her wake the Pomeranian
A favourite of octogenarians
Attired in outmoded astrakhan
Clutching a bag with bejewelled hand
A rope of pearls on her bosom sits
Genuinely developed from oyster grits
Pince-nez swinging on a gold chain
But all is safe on this old dame
For granted it is taken
All is only imitation.
Relations will check their irritations
With her foibles and regimentation,
The snuffling, wheezing dog at meals
And when his bladder over-spills,
The prize, a 'will' tucked in a bureau
Its copy held by Hope, Hope & Co.
Momentarily a twinge of conscience when Aunt's laid low
Then shrugged off with bravado
Well! 'That's life don't cha know.'
But the last laugh came
From wily Great Aunt Jane
Bequeathing all to a dogs' home and Pomeranian!

Queenie Marshall

Almost Numb

I've tried controlling my emotions
And managed pretty well for me,
I've bound them up, applied the lotions,
These feelings longing to be free.
I've drank the draught and once again
Each hour I dutifully take the analgesic,
Now the pain is something like a dullish ache
But where's the joy and where's the laughter,
The living, feeling part of me,
The stomach ache that follows after laughing uncontrollably.
Come back pain, I'm all forgiving,
Cut me with your sharpest knife.
Now I'm feeling, now I'm living,
Now I know I'm part of life.

Lyn Ellis

Kindred Spirit

My kindred spirit
Speak with me!
Do I embarrass you?

Maybe it's because, I perceive
Your many colours
Shining true.

Your soul's identity, so well hid
From blinded eyes to see
But now you know,
That I see too!
And I know you see me.

Lindsey Susan Powell

The Gift

I write a cheque and send it off.
a present with a note to say 'Spend it on you -
a massage or a pretty dress,
a play, a piece of music or just a meal for two.'

I feel a rush of pleasure,
I see her in my mind
just open up the envelope
with joy that someone has been kind.

She must have got it yesterday
but phone calls there are none.
No word of thanks, no cry of joy,
no sharing of surprise or pleasure
the fun of giving gone.

Its incidental to her day
a silly woman sends her gifts,
a nuisance what to say.
Cash the cheque. Forget it,
carry on the day.

A little flush of happiness
is crushed and peters out.
I wonder if she got it?
I'd never like to ask.

Why bother? What's the use?
Deflated, sad, I shed a tear
the gift is never mentioned
but it festers in my heart.

Wendy Mulville

Many, Many Years Ago

Many years ago,
There were no newspaper, no telly, no radio
But only by word of mouth
News would spread about.

People would daily meet
On roads or city streets
And word would get around
Out of city and out of town.

Now there are so many better ways
That news is spread today.
Just turn on your telly or radio
Hear the things you want to know.

Turn into any station,
Get the information
Get the news
Or whatever you may choose.

If you prefer
You can buy any newspaper.
There are so many things to read
Our eyes you can scarcely believe.

There are so many handy telephones
You can give someone a call
Whether near or far
You can send a telegram
To folks in other lands.

So easy it is today
To speak to someone - near or far away.
You can write letter too
So many things that you can do
It is not like many years ago
When there were no newspapers, telly or radio.

Samuel Grizzle

The Forest

Shadows coyly flit o'er dappling fronds,
Ne'er aware of beauty, nature didst a'glean;
Such fine display for those who stand afore,
In breathless wonder of such splendid scene
No painted canvas couldn't recapture - true,
The magic there portrayed for me and you.

Trees of towering majesty sublime, ensure
To reach aloft; attempt to kiss a sky of azure-blue
With cotton candy clouds adrift.
Darting and seeking fingers - bright, from brilliant orb above
That sweet-caresses soaring realms of leafy-green,
Touching thereupon, akin to lovers, with mingling sheen.

Diamonds wouldst inferior-be to rippling streams;
Such vainless drift o'er glisten'd stones below,
The depths extolling fleeing rays from kissing sun.
Couldst-then a soul true-gaze upon more wondrous content
Than paradise, which sprinkled o'er with 'Angel-Dust'
Be deemed as straight from Heaven sent?

To and fro twixt lefty tracts so high,
With rapturous sound - so swift of wing,
The birds of multicoloured hue do sweetly sing,
Instilling now their praise of nature all around.
Wouldst it not be honest-then, to full embrace
The essence of such glorious place?

E'en should angels strive to magnify such gifts;
Attempt to fine-enhance such scenes as laid a'fore,
'Tis God alone who wields the brush
And lays the final touch 'pon canvas now.
Couldst it be, that even angels' sweetly smile to fair-recall
The works of art which are displayed . . . for one and all?

Dennis F Tye

Everlasting Silences

The rambler rambling perhaps in more ways than one
Walking out in no rain but also out in no sun
Away from all traffic sounds, away from all fears
The view all around, tree and fields as past cloudy sky clears.

In some parts of the sky evermore patches of grey
He wishes the glorious sun would shine and the clouds would go away
But then ever changing new clouds quickly appear
But no rain comes nor are people around who he should fear.

But dark rain-filled clouds to the west give apprehension
And not knowing the landscape, who is about it leads to some tension
Not dressed to take rain and walking the uneven terrain
If he fell and twisted an ankle would he get home in such pain?

He mused that not knowing the time of home arrival
That for safety and assurance of his own survival
On such explorations in rural isolation
Carrying a mobile phone would minimise such desolation.

Dangerous war-torn places he'd seen on TV
Far away landscapes the only way he'd see
So many tragic lives of anguish pain and strife
He could only thank God for his contrasting, sheltered life.

In contrast, he thought young soldiers in Afghanistan losing their lives
Leaving whole families grieving, mothers, fathers, children, wives
But in his dark sky, deserted safe corner of the world
Where the everlasting silence, its tranquillity, another world.

People down on Earth, alone, baffled, crushed and failing
And far away over distant seas far worse and much wailing
There, after the bombs, the guns then follows a dreadful quiescence
Where is the divine intervention the sign of a God's presence?

He feels acutely those eerie oppressive everlasting silences
Everlasting, ominous, everlasting silences
Just as in centuries old paintings the silences are there just the same
Whoever or whatever created all and put us here never reveals its game.

All this was in the poet's mind as he quickly walked
And to the only one who would listen it was to himself he talked
Instead of divine intervention, frustration, tension he tenses
When all of a sudden nothing happened, he suddenly senses.

Yes, why does it seem that we are deserted here alone
Some ill and struggling others no one to talk to no one linked to a cosmic phone
When all of a sudden amidst the oppressive silence all around
Absolutely nothing happened again the second time around.

Gerald Walden

Deep Lines (Aged)

Deep lines etched my age I cannot lie
You glance at me and hurry by
I dance and bow while others preen
Dressed in my lacy summer green
My leafy boughs reach to the sky
To brush the clouds as you pass me by
Dark and warm my roughened bark
Etched by the seasons who leave their mark
You look, but do you see as you hurry by
Or hear my gentle whispered sigh
As you on the back of time pass on
I stand in full view silent an age bygone.

Sheila Pharo

The View From The Balcony

How oft will I remember when time claims his countless dues
And restless soul no longer seeks this loveliest of views
In sadness I soon must leave thee for my native shore
And though I may not see thee I shall love thee evermore.

N'ere must my mind forget the shrouding mist of dawn
That veils the hills and sea in silent mystery
Kissed by first faint rosy light, herald of day newborn
Awaiting the glorious fiery throng to ride in solemn majesty
Hiding soft wraiths adieu in silken fold on fold
When a flood of wondrous light clothes all the world in gold.

No white-capped spray in lively mood protest the stubborn rocks
Prim against the azure sky Valletta broods her seething flocks
Soundless across a sapphire harbour as a city long since dead
Shabby in relentless sun yet a wealth of diamonds for her bed
Even the massive ships seem in slumberous repose
Guarded by aged bastions where sea and sky meet close.

In never-ending search I send my weary sight
Lest perchance I lose but one small detail
Sparkling wings of pigeons in undulating flight
Labouring dghajsa, swift sure launch, the line of yachts full sail.

To have seen such perfect sunset my sight is surely blest
E'en though memory fail and deny me all the rest
Long shadows give each dwelling place
A mellow light and softer face
No artist's palette could bestow such myriad colours as now glow
Crimson, pearl, turquoise, gold, each trying to surpass
Their own reflected glory smiling from the mirrored glass.

Marie Blackburn

Standing By The Rough Stone Wall

Wind strewn leaves, a starlit sky,
Dark that is not dark
Light no light
Reveals
Two cloaked figures
Standing by the rough stone wall.
Who are they
Cloaked;
One grey head, one black
Conferring;
Earnest in gesture,
Gentle in persuasion?
Would grey head persuade black
To something he misliked
To ease a burden
He could not support alone?
Or do they speak at ease
Of things they understand
At peace in prayer,
And gently gossip on the times,
On passers-by, of this and that,
In light no light
In dark
That is not dark?

Anne Oakley

Skylight

From my bed
My skylight
In daylight
Frames a skyscape
Of flying clouds
Glimpses of blue
And squares of sunlight
Sometimes trails of rain.

But one night
Waking and turning my head
My skylight
In night light
Frames a skyscape
Of black night
With one single
Bright
Pin bright
One only light
One star
A tiny speck
Of dust light
From eternity
Just one star
Framed
By my skylight
Fixing my gaze
Stilling my heart
Catching my breath
Filling my mind -
A wondrous epiphany.

Anne P Munday

Always And Everywhere

Although I go before you,
Don't let your heart be sad,
Think of all the fun and laughter,
The happy times we had.
The years we spent together
With family all around,
The links remain unbroken,
The ties by which we're bound.

If a sadness makes you ask why
I was not allowed to stay,
Think of me and you will find
That I am never far away.
You may feel me in the sunshine,
See me in the stars above,
When the new life comes in springtime,
Remember me with love.
The love that burns so brightly,
The love that we still share,
Just remember I am with you
Always and everywhere.

Stuart Powell

Celebrations

Come on everybody,
Have you heard the news?
Forward Press are celebrating,
Anyone got a clue?
Well, they have all been working
For the good of you and me,
To publish all our poetry
For the world to read.
And as the time has flown by
The staff cannot believe,
They're celebrating their birthday
And what a party it will be.
For 21 years in publishing
What a brilliant feat,
No talk of a recession
In keeping them of their feet.
So get a glass of bubbly
And together we will rise
To toast the work of Forward Press
Forever may it thrive.

Sharon Eastmond

Walk With Me

Walk with me through bluebell-bedded forest glade
Filtered sunlight shafts catch tangled undergrowth in dappled shade
Birdsong whistle in harmony with whispering breeze in leaf canopy.

Walk with me through warm, soft, sinking, sandy shore
Trickle and tickle of waves between your toes on pebbled floor
Vast expanse of sky and sea merge to horizon of infinity.

Walk with me through fields where glistening dew fall lays
Fruitful hedgerows crowned with silk spun silver strands in misty haze
Gusty wind shakes laden trees, fire-flamed leaves drift earthwardly.

Walk with me through icing topping virgin snow
Fingers numb in frozen air, tingling toes, icy cheeks aglow
A newly painted winterland, light reflected, muted sound.

If all the wishes in the world would set me free
I would walk with you just like we used to do, you and me
Do dreams really come true? Maybe they do, some day.

Shirley Clayden

Grand Prix Celebration

On the podium
the winner pops the cork,
spraying the spectators,
and letters - not bubbles - fly out:
consonants and vowels,
block letters and small,
upper case, lower case,
call them what you will -
falling and tumbling
around the watching journalists
who scramble for this unexpected shower
of alphabet confetti
just waiting to be turned
into copy for the next day's news.

Bea Ewart

Memories At Christmas Time

I have a list of folk I know, all written in a book,
And every year at Christmas time I go and take a look.
And that is when I realise that these names are a part,
Not of the book they're written in, but of my very heart.

For each name stands for someone who has crossed my path some time
And in that meeting there became the rhythm in each rhyme,
And while it sounds fantastic for me to make this claim
I really feel that I'm composed of each remembered name.

And while you may not be aware of any special link
Just meeting you has changed my life a lot more than you think
For once I've met somebody new the years cannot erase
The memory of a pleasant word or of a friendly face.

So never think my Christmas cards are just a mere routine
Of names upon a Christmas list, forgotten in-between,
For when I send a Christmas card that is addressed to you
It's because you're on a list of folks that I'm indebted to.

For I am but the total of the many folks I've met
And you happen to be one of those I prefer not to forget
And whether I have known you for many years or few
In some way you have had a part in shaping things I do.

And every year when Christmas comes I realise anew
The best gift life can offer is meeting folks like you
And may the Christmas season and its spirit which endures
Leave its richest blessings in the hearts of you and yours.

Maureen Alexander

A Walk In The Woods

I walked in shadows beside a rippling stream,
and overhead a canopy of leaves so dense.
I lift my eyes as if awoken from a dream
to spears of sunlight dazzling my sense.

I stop to wipe away involuntary tears;
my blurring vision shocked by bright sun's ray.
An old oak of indeterminable years,
became my crutch my refuge and my stay.

Then, as my eyes allowed me to walk on
I saw with clarity such greens, and rusts and blues.
There all around, beneath, above and yon
a myriad of oh such lush and wondrous hues.

Carpets of bluebells, beech leaves, acorns green.
Coloured fungi grows on rotting logs and tree.
White death caps amid grass tufts are seen
And here and there are wood anemones.

Except that leaves are softly stirring, all is still.
Hushed in trees, the nesting birds on high.
Silent now, the tapping of the woodpecker's bill.
It seems the very woodland waits till I pass by.

Out into sunlight I leave the wood behind
To pause a moment listening, I turn around
The woods now free from trespasser, mankind
Is now all movement and a wild cacophony of sound.

James Stuart

Lost Loved One

I recognised your love for me for many years
In-between us we shed a lot of tears
The long married life you spent with me
I prayed for good health but it was not to be
It's then that we got closer together
I was prepared to look after you forever.

The time we spent together I valued a lot
The love and happy times I have not forgot
Although you were sometimes in great pain
Your love and sense of humour stayed the same
So I pray to God to help me through
The dark days without your love thinking of you.

Please God look after him enfold him in Your love
I hope one day we will meet again in Heaven above
Still feeling our presence very close to me
I feel your breath upon my cheek in my mind I see
With the happy memories to help me through
To face the future years alone without you.

Suzanne Tucker

Two Meals

while on holiday
in the north-east
of England
on one day
we went for two meals

the first was at
supposedly the best
fish and chip restaurant
in the country

we had to queue up
to get in
had to share a table
and the staff
were rude and abrupt
as though they had
so many customers
they couldn't give a toss
whether we
were there or not

as a vegetarian
I ordered one of very few
non fish items
- baked beans -
with my chips
and asked if I could
have an egg too
to which I was told
'I'll ask but
you won't get one'
and I didn't

the chips were
thick and chunky
and I asked my friend
if it was the fish
that the restaurant
was famous for
as I'd had better chips
on my local market
at a quarter

of the price
or even my home-made
ones

the second meal
was at a
'tea rooms and antiques'

we were politely
escorted to a table
by the window
with large
comfortable armchairs
and a chandelier
hanging over the table

we ordered tea and cake
and the tea -
mine containing
orange, cloves and cinnamon -
came in a plastic container
half full of delicious
smelling leaves
and was 'poured'
by fitting the container
to the top of the cup

the cake I selected
was lemon and raspberry
which was fresh
soft and flaky
and contained real raspberries
all served with a smile

as for the antiques
I can only assume
that they were
the furniture
the staff
and some of
the other customers
of the two meals
I much preferred
the latter

Colin Cross

Happy 21st 2010

T wenty-one years of age this year, well done!
W ith all of your anthologies to date,
E very new poet had a chance, bar none.
N ew and old poets, writing for their fate
T he Forward press encouraged all to write.
Y our poems and your writing they would scan.

O nly the best they would choose, not the trite
N ow everyone tries the best that they can
E ven some children saw their work in print.

Y es, it's great to see such talent around
E ach poem published makes authors' eyes glint.
A ll poets have ideas and words abound
R ight through these twenty-one years, like a tree,
S trong and withstanding and completely free.

Doreen Ranson

In Quest Of Redemption

Sometimes at night I dream
I return to the past
And put right anything that went wrong
That like Superman I shall soar
Above the heavens and vanquish
The forces of evil once and for all
Then cruel Fate challenges me,
'You've ruined your life,' he says,
'All you can do now is make the
Most of the years left,'
And I awaken numb and chilled.
Let me state that if ever
I have offended anyone's sensibilities
I here and now apologise
And likewise if anyone has hurt me
You are forgiven.
May your light now shine in my life
And mine in yours
For you the reader
Are more precious than gold.

Nigel Evans

The Fallen Heroes

Do we remember then?
Even if we have never met them?

Just a poppy
Or a flag.
That they once stood and saluted,
It is very sad.

An uncle not met,
A father who was wed
Are a memory of wars long ago.
But their photos remind us that they have gone
But in our hearts they linger on.

Of men who died for us to survive.
A terror that could have destroyed so many more lives.

In many ways we remember them with wistful smiles
And hearts full of pride.

FJ Doe

Laura

I stare at you in wonder
My heart bursting with love
I can't believe you're really here
I send a prayer to Heaven above
Could it be I'm dreaming?
Please don't wake me if I am
I just can't believe that today I became a gran
Two big blue eyes staring up at me
I stare into them and melt instantly
My granddaughter, my world.

Sandra Leach

This Wonderful And Mysterious Thing Called Love

Philosophers, poets and musicians write about love,
That transforming power from above;
It started with Adam and Eve,
It has been continued with so much zeal;
A motivating force throughout history,
This is a man and a woman with the chemistry.

I do not know what it is that makes me feel this way,
I only know that I want it to stay;
Never felt this way before,
But I want to feel this way for evermore;
It may have come into my life late
At last I have found my soulmate.

I never thought it would happen to me,
I said it was a dream or just a fantasy;
But you must have a dream of what will suit you,
If you want a dream to come true;
It is all worked out by divine plan,
Man needs woman and woman needs man.

Robin Robinson

I Guess I Am

There they sat in tobacco haze
Guitars were strummed, rifts were played,
All older now but still remained
That ardent urge to entertain.
There sat George his studio
The other guys would come and go,
He just down from far cloud nine
Played his sitar beating time.
There sat Tom craving more beat
Moving to rhythm in his seat,
Good Jeff Lynee enthused for more
Stamped Cuban heels on littered floor,
There sat Dylan keen, but distant still
His nasal twang sharp and shrill.
As they came to end of piece
In tattered shorts hating the LA heat,
Came Olivia Harrison into room
Bemoaning of the nicotine gloom,
Looks at George through worried eyes
Though all protest thrusts windows wide,
Food and drinks strong coffee
Old Bobby with his herbal tea.
As mist escapes from smarting eyes
Sits a pale-faced man they idolized,
In mourning-black with tinted shades
Coming to the end of travelling days.
Dylan drawls to all will that do?
The idol speaks one more play through,
As tapes are changed, spools rewound
Olivia meekly moves around,
Settles by the one they all admire
All Travelling Wilburys from afar.
'Roy,' she says and feels a little child
With pale set face the great man smiles,
'Would you mind, say if you do
Could I a question ask of you?'
His words are few, 'Go ahead mam'

Olivia takes his pale manicured hand,
'When it comes to singing, so they say
You're the best singer alive today.'
He squeezes gently her soft hand
'Thank you mam, I guess I am.'

John Cates

Maturity

Speed of advance is slow
but humanity must grow - and glow
perhaps in future lives
as torment by past ages fade
for humankind must ripen
how big are we in size;

yet possess the means
to lay bare God's Earth.

Should love and sing
quiet tune of other cultures
on our planet
and find the line most never cross.

Herbert Wilson

A Spaniel Wanting Sausages

You watched my every move
As I turned
The sausages over on the grill pan.

Without a sound
You told me your greatest hope
To get more than just the smell.

Careful not to get underfoot
To be sent away
Banished.

Brown eyes pleading
Don't forget me
The uncertainty.

Waiting for the cooking
Cooling down.

The joy of getting a whole sausage . . .
Gone in seconds.

Nicola Grant

Forever (A Paradise For Birds)

At the bottom of my garden
Sits a table for the birds
And on it sits a ring dove all alone
It comes both night and morning
And it coos its own sad song
Hoping, wondering, why its partner does not come
Its partner's dead, I saw it
And I sadly picked it up
It sat within my hands and breathed its last
But I cannot tell the other one
It wouldn't understand
That its happy airborne days
Are all now past.
I love to have the wild birds
Come home each night to feed
But I hate it when they come back here to die
I wish their life all happiness
All sunshine and soft seeds
I wish there was a hole up in the sky
Where dying birds could just fly through
When they had had their day
To the lush and heavenly plains far up above
Where air gun pellets, there are none
Or dangerous hungry cats
And the birds could just bask in each other's love
Forever.

Mary Howell

Right Number Of Friends

The right number of friends is essential
to prevent you from having a social fall
too many of them confuses and complicates
how often you see each of your 'mates'
when your diary's chock-a-block with dates
you're sure to have put too much on your plate
take stock and empty some of your conviviality crate
you'll be glad one day you reduced your socialising rate.

Lots of 'mates' can cause a strain
racing through life's fast lane
unless you reach a partying peak
you can't see them all in one week
if you're lucky you might just see them all within a month
but in this case, there's so many they must be acquaintances
I bet these relationships lose their fizz
for, I reckon as a rule most of them are superficial

A bucket load of 'mates' is an unhealthy state
if you're out with someone different every night
you're not giving your body a chance to recuperate
one day you might see the light
before you slide down and it becomes too late.

I think it's best that you put each friendship to the test
once everyone has been completely assessed
it's time to elbow the cuckoos in the nest.

When you've got just a few friends
you always know where you stand
they never think twice to offer you a helping hand
they steer you clear of trouble
and help you to safely land
when you've lessened your lavish load
by kicking out the odd time-wasting toad
you can devote more time to those who deserve your road.

Tay Collicutt

Mealtime Memories

We sat together as a family
Always for breakfast, dinner and tea
The table was always laid with care
When all was ready we gathered there

A joint of meat on Sundays
Roast beef, pork or lamb
Cold leftovers always on Mondays
And for tea cake, bread and jam

Dad would always carve the meat
And would sharpen the knife on the steel
Woe betide you if you left your seat
As we all enjoyed the family meal

Chicken and turkey was only a Christmas treat
Collected from the butcher with the gammon and meat
The day of the freezer was yet to come
With the shopping mostly left to Mum

Vegetables always fresh home grown
Organic from seeds patiently sown
Home-made mint and horseradish sauce
And mustard for the ham of course

Apple pie and treacle pud
Oh how I remember it tasting so good
We never knew takeaways and burger bars
And drive in meals consumed in cars

While my children have now flown the nest
With these modern times I'll try my best
I shall do what I have always done
Though my table is just laid for one.

Sheila Fry

Girl Rescue

Flints glint silver platinum patina
watching sky cumulus, dark gaps gloom
mood indigo
black trees sway, reach for the sky.

Sheep dot cream the umber hill
gather and rush as they come:
the golden girls for their treat
longed for not to be put off
by windwarning - for they are to the beach

where flints coated in blue white masks,
various pebbles from shorealong
belemnite, ammonite
might add to their collecting

before they try the snot-green sea
splash or paddle or swim way out
to where chalky water gives way to grey
and waves wash toward the west.

Current carries. Strive to get back
to the bend of the beach where they'd gone in
gone - dashed away.

Lightning lights their blondlocks
trailing with seaweed on water's rim
thunder drowns the moans.

But someone has seen from the harbour wall;
lobsterpot fishing boat pushes out
gunwales soaked, propeller tangled
he reaches out a pot

fingers cling to tarry mesh
two at a time he lifts them in.
Six golden mermaids silver with scales.

They flip their soles on the sodden boards
and hug the man at the landing steps
where slinky sun makes iris arch
over crowds huddling to watch
bent with hail and curiosity.
'You'm had a good catch there, skipper!'

Shirley Beckett

Facile Thoughts

Agnostics seldom rouse disdain
Because their honest doubts invite
Respect. But people, self-assured,
Declaring God is dead, is slain
By science on the march, are bore
At least; presumptuous as well.
As science on its own cannot
Observe or else infer, explore
The grounds for faith in Christ. As, based
On person's stumbling talk of what
Their infant soul receives they find
That futile words and thoughts are faced
With task of telling what's perceived,
With little more than bungling sketch
Of depths they've only just begun
To plumb. The deepest love conceived
By man does not begin to touch
The love that springs form God, for whom
Our finest arts are merely works
Of children trying more than much
To only sketch the crudest daub.
And yet they're often nearer truth
Than masterpiece in Tate. Their sense
Of wonder shown at what our orb
Displays of diverse scenes and things,
From breaking waves to creatures large
And small, reveals a pure delight
That gives the soul a sense of wings.
Despite the ceaseless strife beneath
The beauty seen, despite the pain
And tides of tears, there seems to be
A sense of purpose underneath.
To argue otherwise belies
Belief. It offers night instead
Of light, declares that man in end
Is merely corpse consumed by flies.

Henry Disney

Berkhamsted Castle Fete

Fragments of wall, of flint, do stand,
Like icebergs hard and grey,
From out of a rolling grassy sea,
Fresh breeze makes willows sway.

A cottage stands within the bounds,
A guardian of histories sleep,
Behind, a mound with wooden steps,
That once did bear a keep.

Steep banked sides of fickle moat,
Encircle the sunny green,
One more year, the fun of the fete,
Of Berkhamsted, can be seen.

A white marquee for cups of tea,
Fresh buns and sticky cakes,
Dotted about on old tin trays,
Biscuits, on old chipped plates.

A rotary man, from the Inner Wheel
Inflating balloons for their flight,
Writing on names, then trying on tags,
With children spellbound at the sight.

Red dented tins on a rickety rack,
The vicar takes aim with a cheese,
A chance to air a destructive streak,
Contrary to his reverend theories!

Out of the blue, an announcement or two,
Crackling from green battered speakers,
'At quarter to two, to entertain you
The Berkhamsted band of Saint Peter's.'

Meanwhile in a ring, an extraordinary thing,
Nippers are herded like sheep,
In costumes they've seen, but not very keen,
And the youngest are falling asleep.

It's all very nice and cheap at the price
Yet the purpose is not very clear,
Just waiting around for 'hair' to come down,
Sadly no one is licensed for beer.

Last look around the old castle ground,
The crowd are beginning to go,
So many places and so many faces,
Yet rarely a face that you know.

The sun's getting low, soon I will go,
Pleasant journey, on foot, to my home.
I came with an end, to meet a girlfriend,
I will leave, as I came, on my own.

Taking my leave, I do firmly believe.
It will be as it always has been.
One more year the fun of the fete
Of Berkhamsted I have seen.

Colin C Hartup

An Unforgettable Meal

One cannot imagine a picnic without food
From parties or festivals food you can't exclude
At this particular table there was a simple spread
There is a special mention of unleavened bread

As twelve sat down for their evening meal
Their pious leader broke bread and began to reveal
The impending betrayal, as they drank the wine, a symbol of His blood
Which would be shed for others for the word to spread
They denied it all and some were depressed
'No need for your disquiet and unrest'
He said, 'It has been written and so shall it be done.'
So this meal, though only eaten by twelve
Is remembered by millions who on this Earth dwell
And in this way a simple deal
Is recalled and magnified, an unforgettable meal.

Foqia Hayee

Come Dear Friend Let's Play

Come dear friend let's play, make music awhile,
Forget all cares and worries for a day,
Slow airs and waltzes, jigs to make one smile.
Come dear friend let's play.

Power of expression can reach new heights,
With musical language, we cannot fail,
Purity of sound is within our sights.

No ostentation but panache and style,
Sweet melodies and harmonies display,
Seductive strings together can beguile.
Come dear friend let's play.

Eileen Ward

Book

I picked it up and I loved it,
Each engrossing line developed me.
Oh how I blessed my sight!
I took it to bed with me each night.

She wanted it returned.
I never read it all, it was a shame.
Although I remember a few pages,
I'll never hold that book again.

Ian Davey

The Orphan Lad

It was a stormy winter's night, the gales were howling round,
Black rain clouds were hanging low and flooding on the ground.
I trudged along on my way home, across the old farm track,
When I met a bedraggled little boy, who'd not even got a mac.

I said, 'Young lad you should go home, this is not a night to roam.
He replied, 'I've got nowhere to go - I haven't got a home.'
'Well,' I said, 'come home with me, I'll give you shelter for the night,
Then maybe tomorrow I can help to put things right.'

He readily agreed to this, so off we went together,
We walked and talked the whole way home, oblivious to the weather.
When we reached my cottage, I opened up the gate,
I said, 'Young lad, how old are you?' He replied, 'Just eight.'

The next thing that he said to me, caused me to shed a tear,
He said he'd never known his dad and his mother died last year.
Once indoors he removed his wet clothes, and I ran a nice hot bath,
Then he wrapped up in a dressing gown and I sat him by the heart.

I got the lad a nice hot drink, then made sure he was fed,
And then I got some blankets out and made him up a bed.
Next day I took him shopping, to get some clothes to wear,
Then we went to a barber's shop to trim his straggly hair.

I said, 'Young man, to stay with me you'll have to go to school.'
He replied, 'That's what I'd like to do, you'll find that I'm no fool.'
He got on well and studied hard and passed exams with ease
Obtaining several A Levels and many GCSEs.

The lad looked around to find a job, where he could be employed,
And found one in a garage - something he enjoyed!
As time moved on, he met a girl, a pretty little miss.
He said, 'If I get married it'll be to a girl like this.'

The two of them then fell in love, and finally got married
Back at the cottage made their home, over the threshold she was carried.
They later raised a family - a girl and then a boy,
Each time a baby came along it brought us so much joy.

By this time I was getting old, I was getting thin and frail,
But the lad said, 'We'll look after you, we'll do that without fail.'
He said, 'We'll nurse you willingly, right up to the end,
For to me you've been a father, my mentor and best friend.'

Robert Longley

Men In White

Imagine now a country scene,
A Suffolk village with a green.
A village pub, 'The Dove in Flight,'
And fifteen men all dressed in white.
The bowler running, giving all,
The batsman poised to hit the ball.
He lunges with a lofty drive,
The wicket keeper takes a dive.
The bowler leaps just like a cat,
With arms outstretched he yells, 'How's that?'
The umpire stands as still as stone,
Debating whether to condone
And then a finger he does raise,
Without speaking a word or phrase,
The batsman turns and walks away,
He has not scored a run this day.
One side does cheer, one side does not,
For their best bat is out for nought.
Another batsman takes his stance,
Moving feet as in a dance,
He tweaks his bat and smiles with glee,
I'll hit a four, he thinks, *you see!*
The bowler turns and gathers speed
Thundering down just like a steed.
His arm goes up and then goes down
And off the turf the ball does bounce
The batsman strikes, the ball is gone.
At first he thought his stroke was wrong,
Alas, the ball had struck a bump
Then took away the middle stump.
Another cheer to praise success
A sigh from those now in a mess.
The sun had shone upon this day
But to the west the clouds were grey,
And as the rain began to fall
The bowler bowls his final ball.
The batsman makes his final stand
Alas, he's found he first slips hand.

So with the rest he leaves the scene
And now an empty village green.
Upon the green no men in white
They've all gone in 'The Dove in Flight'.

Ian Marsden

A July Day

Remorseless, relentless,
rolling rods of rain,
thrashing, lashing, in a
repetitive refrain.
Cataracts of Heaven,
curtains of misty haze
veil the country landscape
on such dark and stormy days.
Rich green summer colour
concealed and lost from sight.
Now muted silvery greys
appear as though 'tis night.
The heavy lowering sky
gives no hope of release,
no hope of rainbow arc,
or that the torrent will cease.
No other sound is heard
no matter how we strain -
no bird cries on the wind -
just thrashing, lashing rain.

Marjorie Haddon

Nature's Gifts

I love on the warm summer evenings
When the chores are all done for the day,
To sit and relax in the garden
And contemplate nature at play.

The beautiful notes of the blackbird and thrush
As they trill out their eventide song.
The chattering magpie, the call of the dove
The splash of the fish in the pond.

Fat Harold, the woodpigeon, sits on the fence
Surveying his territory.
He's always around - never goes far,
He was born in our garden's plum tree.

Woody Woodpecker flies in now and then
A wonderful sight to see,
He never stays long just pecks at the nuts
Then hammers our old apple tree!

There's Nutty, the squirrel, a comical cove
Determined all peanuts to claim.
He wrecks our bird feeders but what do we care?
We put them together again!

There's a sweet little mouse we call Hercules
Who lives in the old garden wall.
He comes out at dusk for his biscuit,
He's no nuisance or problem at all.

I watch for the bats as they fly overhead,
The damsel flies dance in the air.
Old Oggie, the hedgehog, will be about soon
He knows that his meal will be there.

As dusk turns to darkness, I start counting stars,
The moon shines its light through the trees
I stay in the garden till bed beckons me
It calms me and puts me at ease.

The sights and sounds where nature abounds
Give such pleasure and much food for thought.
Nothing could ever replace them
They're priceless, they cannot be bought!

Doris Morgan

I Am Ocean

My journey was long made by ancient lores
From high on mountain top through valleys,
Deep and scarred, I slide in dappled sunlight
Then rush headlong among jungle greens
To then divide and reach my destiny to merge and swell.
I become a force ruled by tides who in their turn are servants of star, moon and
sky.

I've felt the fury of the storm and rode the anger of the wind
Heard souls cry out unheeded their rest disturbed
Then slip beneath the frozen ice to rest in the darkness of an Arctic winter
And there felt the shifting of the earth.

I shelter deadly enemies; I am not judge or jury
They have their place, their time to keep the balance of the planet's meaning
I call and whisper till you remember other places,
Other times and offer gifts of countless treasure only mine that the bottomless
deep surrenders.

I'll nip at toes and tickle knees that frolic in my shallows
But do not trust me; I am dark, moody, restless, deadly
I am a flirt, a lover, a child,
I am me, I am Ocean.

J Hubbard

Just A Smile, Just A Word

Each one of us has days of sadness, days of pain,
Remembrances of those we love and never see again.
Compassion fills our hearts for those the world has sorely tried
And as the troubles mount we feel our hands are firmly tied.

There is little we can do to ease another's care
But just a smile, a friendly word is something we can share
You'd be surprised what this can do to lighten someone's day
And help them onwards through their life when all around seems grey.

So when your life feels drab and sad, just look around and smile
And you will soon find others who respond, and in a while
The feelings that you had of sadness, loneliness or fear
Will ease by sharing just a smile, a word, and may soon disappear.

Lucie Gipson

Cambridge Cottages

Small homes, neat, compact, and roofed with thatch
Adorn the village streets around the land.
Their trim dimensions and their modest height
Betoken craftsmen with a steady hand.

Few rooms in many cases they designed,
But comfortable for families to dwell in peace.
Their gardens, their delight both front and back,
Good soil they till where fruit and veg increase.

From Thorpe and Thorney and Great Abington
To Linton, Grantchester and Ickleton
The village streets and byways offer neighbourly content,
And carefree children still can frolic in the sun.

Flowers bring great pleasure to a happy home,
Their colours bright and radiant in every hue;
Fresh breezes give them further light and tone,
Their placid calm a graceful sight to view.

Sunshine on a cottage in the spring
And summer brings a happy, cheerful feel,
Anticipating harvest and the gathered crops,
Providing folk with many a healthy meal.

Produce may enrich the home
With villages and neighbouring towns replete.
The healthy stock of nearby farms
Yield dairy food and succulent juicy meat.

Tourist and visitors may glean
Some fresh awareness of the rural life
And of contented humble minds, -
An antidote to fear, unease and strife.

The cottage home is often such a gentle place,
Gentle in spirit and a source of pride.
The buildings gleam in pleasant light,
And there's tranquillity where gentle folk abide.

Gwilym Beechey

The Trusty Tools

The trusty tools stand erect and straight
In the old shed by the garden gate.
They have so many tales to tell
Of all the things they do, and fell.
I heard the fork, say to the rake,
'To dig up veg is a piece of cake.'
For which the old spade quick replied,
'I'll take you on, so come outside!'
The rake thought he was best with leaves
But the broom said, 'That's what he believes!'
The mowers both got quite uptight
And thought they both were very bright.
For one was fast, and one was slow
But both thought they should have a go.
Then all the tools came scrambling out
To do their jobs and laugh and shout.
But for all those trusty rusty tools
They really know they are not fools.

P Todd

An Age Old Rhyme Telling Of The March Of Time

There's the shed that is a-fading,
The woodwork needs a painting,
The summerhouse too is just the same
Cos the door is hanging down -
A window's cracked - at that I frown -
No fun now when you're on your own.

Too many lawns - so some had to go
Back won't let me mow them don't you know
Tiled too - hope that'll do - tother side we'll have to chew
No mower - broke - what a to-do.

Conservatory - well, that's a laugh
Let's in enough water to fill a bath!
I totter indoors and take another pill.

Had gas heating installed - I wonder why?
The price of gas is going sky high,
Bay window's now sprung a leak
Builder only plugged it up last week.

Rain again - oh what a year
Finds all the nooks and crannies here.
'When my ship comes home', goes the saying
Well, with all this rain and all my praying
It surely will come by a-sailing
And I live on a hill!

Molly Martin

Progression And Regression

(Musings of a Sexagenarian)

As a child it seemed to me, the world was full of words
Our teachers taught us grammar, the role of nouns and verbs.
The present, past and future tense, perfect subjunctives too
Latin became our Everest the peak of all we knew.
Declensions studied daily, were recited with delight.

Every tool was given us to perfect our prose and verse,
With pen and ink and many a blot, we carefully formed each word
Above each line, across the page, to bring our thoughts in view.
Our spellings though were noted, all errors slashed right through
Hence spelling tests and spelling bees to keep our work unscathed.

My favourite room in childhood cherished my parents' books
Where Tennyson met Churchill, and O'Henry, HG Wells.
Each book advertised its value, by the splendour of its cloth
And each held untold excitement, through discovery by oneself.
How carefully I turned each page, to taste my parents' world.

When I became a mother the book still reigned supreme,
The joys of bedtime reading sparking many a childhood dream.
Each Christmas brought each child a book, selected just for them.
For holidays we'd camp abroad and share our books around
Snuggling up to read them, as summer showers came down.

The digital explosion defined my later years
From DVDs to iPods it had me in arrears.
Information searching grew ever more precise,
Nothing was impossible, just design a new device.
The typewriter left in tatters, as Microsoft took hold.

And now I'm in my sixties and choose how my time is spent
I can Google, text or email until my heart's content.
Oh yes I use computers and wonder at their skill
But the key to my contentment lies, and always will
Between the covers of the books, that tumble from my shelves.

Rosemary Bremer

Changing Moods

I'm gazing out of the window
Thinking of me and you,
Wondering if our love will last
And whether I can stay true.

The rain is falling faster
And running down the pane,
The weather is suiting my mood
My doubts are back again.

I don't feel ready to go steady
How can I let you know?
You say you really care for me
Maybe my love will grow.

With this in mind I feel happier
The sun is shining through,
My heart feels slightly lighter
Because I'm still seeing you.

Brenda Butler

Cromer Carnival

It's Cromer Carnival time once more
    Bigger and better than ever before.
Grannies are flaunting in their high heels
    Dolled-up to the nines, the judges to please.
Men young and old, show their knobbly knees
    A fun day off work, they're really pleased.
Babies are dressed in their Sunday best
    Smiling and cooing for their very first test.
There's catching crabs on Cromer pier
    Don't fall off lads, still the inshore's there.
The waiters and waitresses race along
    Hoping their beer-trays don't land on the prom.
There's darts, snooker, bingo and also quizzes
    Some will win and some have near-misses.
The Red Arrows are performing once again here
    We watch their manoeuvres and skills as they dare.
Then at night that magnificent carnival procession
    Goes through the town in flamboyant succession.
The torchlight parade is dazzlingly bright
    A wonderful sight on a dark, dark night.
As the fireworks explode and light up the sky
    'Alas it's all over,' we say with a sigh.

Leah Everitt

The Age To Dream

(Written on my 90th birthday)

Watching night clouds drifting by
When suddenly the moon appears
Her beams lighting up the sky
I'm old and disabled now
Confined in my room and bed
Thinking of my past achievements
And what lies for me ahead
As the moon slowly wends her way
Her beams lighten up my room
Is she showing me a way to freedom?
Freedom that I yearn
How should I cope with my life
Should I not forget to pray?
To ask my maker just one wish I ask of you
When I pass away
To give my spirit eternal life
To last forever come what may.

Dorothy Gould

If I Had Not Been A Grandad

If I had not been a grandad, growing older and wiser every day,
I might have missed Marnie's poem, seeing what she had to say.
But I am one better, I am hers,
It took me back to my schooldays and all it incurs.
Marnie looks ahead at all that is to come . . .
A farmer, a diver, an actress, it sounds a lot of fun.
It will be and Marnie will do it well
I am old and wise and I can tell
So if you dive or farm or act on the stage
Whatever it is, you'll be all the rage
A word of warning beware of those rocks
Sometimes they can look just like those chocs
We loved your poem, we love you as well
Work hard, you will make it, I am wise I can tell.

Harold Norton

Love

Love is a very special word
It means so much, you must have heard
To care for, admire, trust and peace of mind
Comes all too easy with a heart entwined
Beautiful is the little white dove
To remind us all of the word of love
Being with those that I adore
Love is bliss and you can't ask for more.

Christine Williams

Springtime Again

The robin I saw perched on a fence
Sang to the peasant who courted a wench
Surrounded by hills like emeralds fine
Tall trees quiver as if drunk with wine
The birds take to the air hovering on the wing
It's springtime again, I hear a voice sing.

So step forth and rejoice in the land
And praise to God who took a hand
In giving us this gift so fair
For all mankind to equally share
Nature gives her gifts to all
Whether they be short or tall

So let us come and rejoice in our hearts
The loveliness of springtime that plays a part
Of all the seasons that give us our reasons
For living our lives
As husbands and wives
That we are here to complement each other
To love mankind sister and brother.

Jackie Oung

Nicholas

You -
So far away.
Beyond barriers
I cannot reach.
Not walls
Mountains
Seas or land
But time.
So long ago
And far away
You lived your life
Day by day.

I wish
That I
Had lived there too
In that age
So long ago
To know you
See you
Talk to you
As you were
Then!

But perhaps
In fact
You are not
So far away.
Nearer to me
For travel
And time
Is nothing
To you now.
You move
As and where
You will
Swiftly.

And I believe
That every day
You are here
Beside me

Although
I do not
See you
Physically -
Speak to you
With my lips
I talk to you
In mind alone
And see you
In my dreams.

Christina Miller

Sussex - Unforgettable Beauty

Enter the gates of magnificent Sheffield Park
Marvel at the great ponds, bordered reflectively with red, white, purple
rhododendrons
The wind passes over flowers, shake coloured rippling water
Water lilies, red, white, yellow, float abundantly over vast ponds
Swans with their cygnets- caress calm waters
1st Earl de la Warr 1292 planted avenues of oak, ash, walnut, cherry
Famous families also owned gardens, Sackvilles 1623, Nevilles
Thomas Howard 3rd Duke of Norfolk entertained Henry VIII - August 1538 in
gardens

Anne North - wife of Earl 1798 laid out framework of garden
Reflections, breathtaking at the lakes 1896 Australian cricket touring team
Played 3rd Earl's - Lord Sheffield's team
Capability Brown and Humphrey Repton 3rd Earl made famous the Cricket House

1910 Arthur Gilstrap-Soames blossomed the garden
Planting rhododendrons enjoyed by Virginia Woolf
Spectacular autumn colour with Japanese maples,
Beds of autumn gentians

3rd Earl Soames - married Agnes Peel
Grandaughter of Victorian Prime Minister - Agnes devoted her life to the gardens
1987 storm the huge sequoiadendron giganteum-wellingtonia - survived
Sheffield means (sheep clearing) nature's brilliant colours, beauty, a joy to behold.

Patricia Turpin

North Downs

If you are seeking summer - come with me
Along this rising lane, between high banks
Pierced by the roots of silver trees
Pink with tall foxgloves spread in ragged ranks
Awaiting onslaughts from the burrowing bees.
Over the bank - and through the narrow wood
Pass by that path behind its screen of leaves
That must lead on to secret mossy parts
With greener grass and rarer flowers than these.
Not now to watch where small birds start and sing
But rather see the lark rise out the ground
Suddenly - out on the bare grass Down.

Only the blazing high unshaded sun
Sees the Down's end or where it was begun.
Look - all along it falls in pleasances
Toward a land that's boundless-vanishes
Into a haze of smallest woods and fields.
And there below us, like a tidal cliff,
The bare grass Down to lapping culture yields.
Sights and sounds of tiny movements rise:
Carts on the roads, slow cattle in the meadows.
Faint smoke is lost before it meets the sky
And over all the ever swooping swallows
Here is your sought-for perfect summer's day.

Raymond Philo

Norfolk, My Norfolk

Whispering reeds and a mackerel sky,
Light fluffy clouds drifting on high.
Cool lapping water reflecting the blue
Lazily dreaming of days spent with you.

Butterflies flitting from blossom to flower
Somewhere a church clock is chiming the hour.
Norfolk, my Norfolk, this bright sunny morn
Sweet glows the red poppy amongst golden corn.

Across on the bank a green willow hangs low
Dipping a branch in the water below
Where stands a tall heron, majestic and still
Waiting to catch the next fish in his bill.

A proud horse in the far field tail-switches a fly
As I quietly watch a small leaf floating by.
Norfolk, my Norfolk, how sweet the sun's rays
Change not your peace for the rest of my days.

Helen E Langstone

Too Late

When the golden sun is shining
over grassland, tree and hill,
When the daffodils are dancing
and all is quiet and still.
When the powdered blue of Heaven
is reflected in the lake,
Then a magic spell is woven
that no one should dare to break.

There's a loveliness in nature
that cannot be made by man,
And it quietly goes on working
in all corners of the land.
Spring, summer, autumn, winter,
all eventually will be,
And it quietly goes on working
all around the human sea.

Yet this spell is often broken
and destruction takes its place,
There's no beauty in a battlefield
or in a pain torn face.
When man no longer cares about
the loveliness around,
To gain more power, to fight, to kill
to mutilate the ground.

But when the guns are quiet again
the bombs have done their worst,
The dust has settled on the land
so wretched and accursed.
Upon a pile of rubble
the grass begins to grow,
The tiny daisies soon appear
the bees are on the go.

So Mother Nature once again
begins her magic spell,
To cover up the dirt and dust
proclaiming all is well.
But if, one day, maybe, perhaps
when man has done his worst
No more will Mother Nature come

the land will stand accursed . . .
Forever and forever,
Too late to change our way,
Too late to stop, to start to think,
Destruction here to stay!

Sandra J Walker

The People's Publisher

Wow, 21 today
Forward Press
Has come of age
And all that publishing
To get our work
Printed on a page.
They've broken down
The barriers
To get our work to print
Over one million
Already published
Wow, what a lot of ink!
I'd like this poem
Of mine printed
To say happy anniversary
Forward Press
Thank you for all you do
I send my poem
And you do all the rest.

Diana Stopher

The Unscrupulous MPs Of Whitehall

Unscrupulous MPs of the present and the past
They have been caught and found out at last.
Of their shady dealings here and there, the population
Of this country for so long unaware.
Thanks to the Daily Telegraph has brought assumed perks to light
And how it has put the MPs in such an awful plight.
It is disgraceful that it has been going on for so long
I hope one day swift justice will soon come along.
Some MPs have paid back in shame as they worried about their fame
I wonder what future revelations will come about
For again the population in anger may shout.
With the elections that are coming in a year or so
The MPs have a lot of work to do to extract themselves from this terrible stew.
So here ends my tale of the MPs' sorrow and hope
In the end there will be a brilliant to-morrow.

Peter Antonian

One Day

One day I will grow strong enough to hold your essence in my hands
I will emerge from this numbness and feel the silk of your skin
And when I cannot, they will bury me in your arms
And the warmth of you will turn my body to ash
My hair will turn to flame and I will crumble into cinders
You will put me in an hour glass and I will spend eternity upside down trying to
return to you.

One day I will grow wise enough to see you in front of me
I will rise up through floorboards and through cracks in walls and rest my head on
your shoulders
And you will touch me with acknowledgement
And when I cannot the storm of your eyes will swallow me
It will engulf me in its glittering battling sea
And I will float down to the seabed and wait there
Waiting until you release me
Releasing oxygen bubbles of prayer from my mouth that you should not
Thankful that I have drowned.

One day when I am old, time will blunt the jagged sharpness of life
I will grow wild-eyed and mad and dance around the kitchen
And I will believe I am dancing with you.

Sophie Aaronson

The Huntress

Lithe and agile
The sleek black cat jumps on to the garden bench
She crouches, watching,
Flattens herself so she is almost one with the wood
Black tail dangling -
The gently flicking tip the only movement,
Green eyes gleaming
Gaze fixed on a blackbird in the apple tree.
Suddenly, she leaps
Like a black torpedo she launches into the air
Misses completely.
The bird moves to a higher branch,
The cat scratches her ear.
Then sits beneath the tree washing her paws,
Feigning disinterest.
She looks round
Nobody seems to be watching
She stretches
Wanders away towards the kitchen door
There may be food in her dish
If not
A quiet sleep in the afternoon sun
Dreaming
Of all the hunting she could do
If only she had the time!

Maureen Lejeune

On Re-Hearing Vaughan Williams
'The Lark Ascending'

Clean,
Pale green
And blurry, blue-shot gold,
Soaring,
With
Heartbreaking, hovering clarity,
To skies
Far brighter than my soul,
Far lighter than my heart . . .
This music,
This violin-borne lark-song
Returns me
My England of a better day,
Where I, cornfield-dawdled,
Warm - grass - snuggled
And was safe, where
Shining mornings,
Hung with larks like this
And hot-eyed, heavy daisies
Promised me
Only
The high,
The sweet,
The good,
The pure . . .
Forever and forever.

Edna Harvey

Coming Of Age

A babe in arms cradled in unconditional love,
A gift so special sent from the angels above.
But at two not so meek, with my favourite word, 'No!'
By four new boundaries to push, so many places to go.
Come five it was school with numerous new faces,
Cardigans with buttons and tricky shoelaces.
Drawing and crayoning with teacher to please,
Doing reading then arithmetic with relative ease.
Exams for the 11+ with scary horizons looming,
Everything hingeing on the learning I'd been consuming.
Formal attire for the first day of term
Friendships and memories for eternity affirmed.
Growing through adolescence with malice and spite,
Groaning, moaning, complaining, never getting it right.
'How can you treat me like a child when I'm nearly fifteen?'
Hurt, tears pained with rejection by a sweet boy of sixteen.
In time, life's opportunities lie impatiently ahead
Independence and the vote but by Mum's hand I'm still fed.
Joyous, triumphant I find a place of my own
Jubilant, jubileum my first Christmas alone
Kind words embrace me and my 'Coming of Age'!

Pamela Hayman

Song Of The Mountain Stream

In echoing caves and crystal pools,
Where glaciers weep, my song is born,
Through mosses fresh from winter's sleep,
My theme has turned to gentleness.

Across high meadows dressed in snow,
Soft murmuring voices join with mine:
I spread my arms to gather in
Each joyful note, each kindred theme.

Till gathering pace in giddy leaps,
Down through the stone strewn way I speed,
Vaulting great rocks in breathless haste,
Heady at my power, my song

Crescendo in my new found strength.
Nothing can slow this white winged flight
Through deep cut valleys. Now my voice
Booms, echoing from high walls.

But then I feel the drag. The rocks
Have gone; white water turned soft green.
My pace, still swift, I glide through banks
Of willow woods and lush meadows.

My lusty song now stilled. Dull sounds
Threaten the silence of my course,
So different from those mossy ways
Left once so joyfully on heights

I will not ever see again
And yet those heady waters drunk
So eagerly, the leaps, the thrills,
The risks have formed my present self.

In these dark draughted depths, no fears
Can silence now my voice. My song
I'll sing, to all its richness tuned;
It shall be mine down to the sea.

Derek Lucking

Lunar Poem

(To celebrate the 40th anniversary of the landing of Apollo Eleven)

Trod by Man in recent times
This lonely orb holds ancient signs,
Apollo came and lightly landed,
Sampled, tested, US branded.

Yet is it cheese or Man in moon?
Our romance by its silvery tune
And nursery rhymes of childish glee,
Swim in our sea of tranquillity.

Its darker side (like ours) is hidden,
The loony madness comes unbidden,
This orb of tidal, natural phases,
Crescent, new and full displaces.

Crater, sea and epic mountain,
Waterless - bereft of fountain,
Floating weightless and serene,
The earth is king, the moon is queen.

Bryan Perry

James, My Beloved Son

(For my sister whose son passed away in 2008)

Where did you go that summer day
When your sprit left and flew away?
Up into the sky so blue
Where the sun you loved looked down on you.
Those chains were broke, you were set free,
But you couldn't know what it did to me.

I cry, I cry, I am so sad,
For I have lost my lovely lad.
My broken heart it will not mend
Because you were my closest friend.
Your room is dark where once was light,
It used to shine throughout the night.

Your jeep stands quietly on the drive,
Oh how I wish you were alive.
It doesn't know you'll not be back,
For it, there's no more roads to track.

Oh God! Why did You take my boy?
He was my only pride and joy.
I know - there is a time to come
When I'll be with you James, my beloved son.

Deanna Day

Devil And Messiah

I remember you aged eight, dressed up for Hallowe'en,
Spock-like ears above a flaming painted face,
Football scarf loitering around your shoulders
And you brandishing a three pronged fork.

Our mirrored thoughts exchanged a devilish grin
Before you swept regally out of my room -
Well even the King of the Underworld must watch -
When Manchester Untied were playing on the telly.

And now, your eighteenth birthday,
You've dyed your hair resplendent red.
A lightning bolt is slashed across your face,
Your brown leather jacket is fluttering a fringe.

You shoulder throw
A glittery scarf some girl has lent you.
As you turn I notice the hint of hairy chest, and yes,
Ziggy Stardust, the Messiah has landed.

Máire Owens

Growing Older

I love to go out dancing
Hopping and bopping all night
But the moment the band stops
My shoes start getting very tight.
Not so many years ago
It would not have bothered me
I would have kept on dancing
Until they locked up with the key.
Now I am a little bit older
Should I take things more slowly?
Oh no, that would be boring
I shall grow old disgracefully
Feeling I have earned the right
Doing things I always wanted to
I may even surprise myself
Who knows what I could do.
I'd love to swim with dolphins
It's certainly not too late
Perhaps take a balloon flight
The possibilities are great.
Try learning another language
Cruise to Alaska to watch the whales
Visit Australia and New Zealand
I would have such terrific tales.
Now I've made my decision
I don't intend to hang around
May even raise a few eyebrows
At the new life for myself I've found.

Judith Watts

If That's How You Feel About It

If that's how you feel about it
We're captured in time
In a large love balloon
Floating in space
Everything will be okay
Everything will be fine

Love one another
Be true to yourself
Be true to one another
Be true to themselves

Have no fear in this world
It's only a farce
Have no fear in anything
It's only time that will pass

Time's never-ending
We'll live eternally
Forever in love
Together we'll be

And if that's how you feel about it
We're captured in time
In a large love balloon
Floating in space
Everything will be okay
Everything will be fine.

Christian Schou

Dreams

Nearly one thousand years ago
the Normans stamped their mark upon this land.
They built cathedrals - dreams in stone that held the sky
and unified the awe and majesty of God
with the permanence of the invaders' dominion.

For near a thousand years our cathedral
dominated this land unchallenged,
until the concrete reality of the sixties
allowed the less imaginative architect
of a more prosaic dream to break the sky
with an office block named Hereward
in reminiscence of the long gone Anglo-Saxon world.

Other dreams have also pierced the sky.
Mosques provide alternative signposts to Heaven
as more recent arrivals from our smaller, wider world
build their dreams in the rich complexities of this city.

But for most people these pointing spires
or high vaulted ceilings no longer hold their dreams.

The new cathedral is Queensgate Shopping Centre.
Half-price sales call them to prayer.
They drive to worship 24 hours a day,
at the low church of Hampton's Tesco's.
Their dreams are of a fuller life measured in acquisition
and celebrated in electronic goods from China.

Steve Walker

My Mum

Dear Mum I miss you so
Since you were taken from us, which wasn't that long ago
Remember how we used to laugh and chat over the phone
You listening, both laughing, but also having the occasional moan
Oh how I miss those days, but you're still with me
Etched deep in my heart
Your generosity, kindness, sense of fun, where do I start?
When I think of you I smile and grateful for the time you were here
Although there are many times I shed a silent tear
I know you're up there somewhat Mum, of that I have no doubt
Having fun, laughing and most probably getting ready to go out
I chat about you often, talking about the past
Your memory is kept alive dear Mum, in my mind, my soul, you will be with me
                                                        until the very last

I could be unhappy and so very sad
But I choose to smile and be grateful for the great mum you were and the happy
                                                        times we had.

Elaine Moore

Pearl Anniversary

Words are used in poems to convey our feelings and thoughts,
Whether it be sadness, or joy, but love is a word that cannot be explained.

Some would say it is a great feeling of jubilation and warmth,
that comes from deep within our hearts.

Today we celebrate our pearl anniversary.
When I stood at the altar and looked into your eyes
I knew then, that the flame I carried for you deep within my heart
would always burn brightly for you.

If our souls were like mirrors
you would see that our love for each other is written in the stars.

Those vows of love that I made then, still stand true today.

Brian Ross

Chance Meeting

I met an old chap, on my way to the town,
He, going home, pushing his shopper.
Me, pushing mine. Made for conversation.
He, ninety-one, me, seventy-five.
Had things in common.
Still, I learnt some facts.
Five minutes passed, we shook hands,
'All the best,' we said.

Pam Hammocks

Time

It fills the faces of every clock
As it squeezes between the tick and tock
We're told, it's precious by the old
But, it takes a lifetime, to unfold
It passes too slowly, for those who wait
But, whenever, we're pressed it makes us late
It slips through fingers when held too tight
But when in pain it ignores our wish, it might
It separates, the present from that of history
While turning our days, with a touch of mystery
And despite the varied paths that are ours to follow
Death will claim back, all that we borrow
We hear it still ticking, through your life and mine
Although much less important, than eternity, defined!

Dennis Thomsett

Urban Landscape

Gloomy grey, leaden black,
a dismal sight to see,
a foggy-like horizon with nothing clear to me.

No sun, no sound,
a misty murky haze,
sulphuric like pollution to send an early grave.

No clouds, no sun,
trees shrivelled up and gnarled,
the beauty of the seasons now much reviled.

I care, do you?
About those yet unborn,
conserve, we must, and not leave them to mourn.

Janet Clare

The Rain In Spain

The day we arrived in Spain,
It started to pour with rain.
The coach broke down to the hotel
When we got there not all was well.
You would never guess what we found,
The whole roof was still lying on the ground!
Manager said not to worry
Pushed us upstairs in rather a hurry.
Our room, well, if you can call it that,
Wasn't even big enough for our cat.
Teatime arrived and yes you guessed,
The meal turned out to be a mess.
After two weeks the rain's still here,
Packing up to go home, who said three cheers?
Now sitting on the plane, regretting we come,
I don't believe it, I can see the sun.

Rose Snape

Forward Press Information

We hope you have enjoyed reading this book - and that you will continue to enjoy it in the coming years.

If you like reading and writing poetry drop us a line, or give us a call, and we'll send you a free information pack.

Alternatively if you would like to order further copies of this book or any of our other titles, then please give us a call or log onto our website at www.forwardpress.co.uk

Forward Press Information
Remus House
Coltsfoot Drive
Peterborough
PE2 9JX
(01733) 890099